THE LIFE
OF OUR
DESIGN

Organization and Related Strategies
in *Troilus* and *Cressida*

VERNON P. LOGGINS

UNIVERSITY
PRESS OF
AMERICA

Lanham • New York • London

Copyright © 1992 by
University Press of America®, Inc.
4720 Boston Way
Lanham, Maryland 20706

3 Henrietta Street
London WC2E 8LU England

Library of Congress Cataloging-in-Publication Data

Loggins, Vernon P., 1952.
The life of our design : organization and related strategies
in Troilus and Cressida / Vernon P. Loggins.
p.   cm.
Includes bibliographical references and index.
1. Shakespeare, William, 1564–1616. Troilus and Cressida.
2. Troilus (Legendary character) in literature.
3. Trojan War in literature.   I. Title.
PR2836.L6   1992   822.3'3—dc20   91–36600 CIP

ISBN 0–8191–8510–8 (alk. paper)

To William B. Bache

Contents

Acknowledgments

This book examines the unity and organization of *Troilus and Cressida*. I owe an incalculable debt to the many critics who have preceded me, and I have attempted to acknowledge this debt in notes throughout the book. I am grateful to the kind people at the Newberry Library in Chicago for providing access to the collection and to Valdosta State College for a Faculty Research Grant to fund study at the Folger Shakespeare Library in Washington, D.C., and I should like to thank the generous people at the Folger. Parts of this book have appeared elsewhere. Kind permission was granted to reprint portions of the following articles: "Rhetoric and Action in *Troilus and Cressida*," *CLA Journal* and "Perspectives in *Troilus and Cressida*," *The Dalhousie Review*. For editorial advice I have had the assistance of my colleague Rick Denton. Finally, I owe a particular debt of gratitude to William B. Bache, who remains my teacher and friend, and to whom I dedicate this book.

A Note On Texts

All quotations from *Troilus and Cressida* are taken from the Arden edition of the works of William Shakespeare edited by Kenneth Palmer, (London: Methuen, 1982). All other quotations from Shakespeare are taken from *The Riverside Shakespeare*, ed. G. Blakemore Evans, (Boston: Houghton Mifflin, 1974). The only substantial departure from these texts is that speech-prefixes are given in full.

Introduction

Although it is not considered Shakespeare's greatest play, *Troilus and Cressida* seems to be Shakespeare's most difficult and most intellectual work. Not surprisingly, the only occurrence in the canon of the word *cognition* appears in *Troilus and Cressida*. The status of the play is problematical. Part of the play's intellectual difficulty is inherent in its subject matter, the Trojan War, and in Shakespeare's treatment of that subject matter. Considering the size and complexity of the subject matter, *Troilus and Cressida* presented Shakespeare with difficult problems that, by virtue of the story of the Trojan War's currency among the Elizabethan audience, must have made this play particularly challenging. As John Tatlock notes, "No traditional story was so popular in the Elizabethan age as that of the siege of Troy and some of its episodes; because . . . of the tradition that the Britons were descendants of the Trojans, a tradition which certainly often determined point of view."[1]

Although Shakespeare chose to deal with a subject matter of singular scope and importance, he proceeded to deal with that subject matter in his usual manner. Thus *Troilus and Cressida* employs strategies used in the other plays as well as strategies particular to *Troilus and Cressida*. Moreover, set within the context of the public, war plot is the private, love plot, which concerns the two titular characters, Troilus and Cressida. In no other play does Shakespeare deal so fully or so thoroughly with love in terms of war and with war in terms of love. But because of the complexity of the dramatic and poetic problem, *Troilus and Cressida* has been much misunderstood. Not surprisingly, criticism has not dealt kindly with the play.

The New Historicists, however, are helping us to see the value of what Stephen Greenblatt calls "the margins of the text."[2] Although, as G. Blakemore Evans argues, critics like Alfred Harbage once maintained that Shakespeare's audience consisted of a wide range of patrons (the public theaters being attended by commoners and the private theaters being attended by more educated and "socially select" patrons), recent criticism by Ann J. Cook determines that Shakespeare's audience was much more homogenous than we had previously thought.[3] This kind of information helps in part to explain why *Troilus and Cressida* is as thoroughly intellectual as it is, its primary audience being at the Inns of Court, as Perter Alexander first theorized.[4] But Stephen Greenblatt also admits that "sustained, scrupulous attention to formal and linguistic design will remain at the center of literary teaching and study."[5]

Thus, and because of the force of received opinion about *Troilus and Cressida*, I find it necessary to begin by considering the play not as an anomaly but as being Shakespearean. I start with the assumption that Shakespeare and his usual procedures will teach us how to read *Troilus and Cressida*. We must deal with the play on its own terms as a Shakespeare play first. If we recognize Shakespeare's patterns, strategies, systems, identify them, and then apply them to the play, essential problems of understanding are resolved. Thus we must first identify and understand those strategies that are Shakespearean and then those strategies that, although Shakespearean in nature, have particular applicability to *Troilus and Cressida*. Let me mention a few large-scale Shakespearean strategies.

In addition to the five-act structure, a Shakespeare play may be said to have two parts. Generally speaking, the first part of a Shakespeare play ends with the third Act and may be said to begin again in Act IV. *Richard II* and *The Winter's Tale* are classic examples of this two-part structure. According to E.M.W. Tillyard, a Shakespeare play may be said to have three stages, *prosperity*, *destruction*, *re-creation*.[6] To refine these terms, we may say that a Shakespeare play begins with *seeming*, moves to *reality*, and concludes with *art*; that is, a Shakespeare play begins with seeming prosperity, moves to destructive reality, and concludes with artist re-creation. We have no trouble seeing the validity of the five-act structure, of the two-part structure, of the three-stage structure in *Troilus and Cressida*. These large-scale formulations instruct our primary approach.

In addition to these structural strategies, however, a Shakespeare play uses three essential tropes: the body, the family, the stage. The body trope involves the head, the heart, the hand, an elaborate metaphor for action qualified by intellect and feeling: the head thinks; the heart feels; the hand does. The family trope is a metaphor for the social unit; the family is a metaphor for society in which each member feels a tension with and an obligation to the larger social unit.[7] Finally, the well-accepted significance of the stage or play-acting trope is a useful Shakespearean notion. Although each of these tropes operates on a level different from that of the others, they are nevertheless interconnected. For instance, in the family trope the father corresponds to the head, the mother to the heart, the children to the hands. Each member of the family plays his or her assigned role, thus effecting the play-acting or stage trope. In other words, although these tropes are part of individual systems of organization, they are not mutually exclusive, and they are not exhaustive.

Although I assume the relevance of general Shakespeare patterns and systems, my concern is for those patterns, strategies, systems that are of service in understanding *Troilus and Cressida*. By identifying these strategies, I hope to make the play clearer and more accessible. And although I do not pretend to offer definitive answers to this most difficult of Shakespeare plays, I hope to uncover what Troilus calls "the life of our design" (II.ii.195), to discover meaning where only problems have been perceived: "all difficulties are but easy when they are known" (*MM* IV.ii.205-06).

NOTES

1. John Tatlock, "The Siege of Troy in Elizabethan Literature," *PMLA* (1915): 673.

2. Stephen Greenblatt, *Shakespearean Negotiations* (Berkeley: Univ. of California Press, 1988), 4.

3. See Ann J. Cook in G. Blakemore Evans, *Elizabethan-Jacobean Drama: The Theatre in Its Time* (New York: New Amsterdam, 1988), 18.

4. See Peter Alexander, *Shakespeare* (London: Oxford Univ. Press, 1964), 248; *Shakespeare's Life and Art* (New York: New York Univ. Press, 1961), 194-96.

5. Greenblatt, 4.

6. E.M.W. Tillyard, *Shakespeare's Problem Plays* (London: Chatto and Windus, 1961), 16-58. I am greatly indebted to William B. Bache for the information contained in this and the next paragraph. See *Design and Closure in Shakespeare's Major Plays: The Nature of Recapitulation* (New York: Peter Lang, 1991), 3-6.

7. D.A. Traversi, *An Approach to Shakespeare*, rev. ed. (Garden City: Doubleday, 1969), 2: 142-43.

1

The Apple of Discord and the Prologue

There is no question about the difficulty of *Troilus and Cressida*.[1] In fact, the genre of no other Shakespeare play is more difficult to identify. As Coleridge remarked, "none of Shakespeare's plays is harder to characterize."[2] The title page of the Quarto calls it a history; the Epistle to the reader refers to it as a comedy. The Folio does not include it in the table of contents. Placing the play after *Henry VIII* and before *Coriolanus*, the Folio seems to consider *Troilus and Cressida* as the first of the tragedies. Since W.W. Lawrence, it has been customary to call *Troilus and Cressida* a "problem play."[3] Unquestionably, it is problematical and difficult.[4]

Part of the play's difficulty is inherent in its subject matter.[5] The Trojan War—which generated the *Iliad*, the *Odyssey*, the *Aeneid*—is a large and complex subject.[6] Its scope is indicated by the Prologue:

> And hither am I come,
> A Prologue arm'd, but not in confidence
> Of author's pen or actor's voice, but suited
> In like conditions as our argument,
> To tell you, fair beholders, that our play
> Leaps o'er the vaunt and firstlings of those broils,

Beginning in the middle, starting thence away
To what may be digested in a play.

(22-29)

Beginning in the middle of the Trojan War, the play is a digestion or condensation of that conflict, as the armed Prologue indicates. Imagine the complexity of a text that reduces a subject of epic proportions to the two-hours' traffic of the stage.

In his introduction to *Troilus and Cressida*, Daniel Seltzer remarks that *Troilus and Cressida* is a "pivotal play,"[7] one that stands at the center of the Shakespeare achievement. It is not one of the early plays, nor is it one of the late plays; it falls between *Hamlet* and *King Lear*. Virgil Whitaker has commented that one cannot be said to understand Shakespeare unless he or she understands *Troilus and Cressida*,[8] the play that presents the greatest challenge to our understanding of any play in the canon. For *Troilus and Cressida* deals with some of Shakespeare's most fundamental concerns: the relationship between lust and violence; the nature of war and the kind of mentality that insures its continuance. Nowhere else does Shakespeare more clearly deal with love in terms of war and with war in terms of love. Yet, like *Romeo and Juliet*, *Troilus and Cressida* involves two families. And like *Antony and Cleopatra*, *Troilus and Cressida* deals with a famous pair of lovers at a crucial public time. As Peter Alexander remarks, *Troilus and Cressida* is sophisticated.[9]

A sophisticated audience would bring to the play a knowledge of the Trojan matter. That audience might expect to hear about heroes and gods. In Shakespeare's account, however, the gods are largely absent. Thus the mythic genesis of the Trojan War, the Apple of Discord, is missing from *Troilus and Cressida*.[10] Like Homer in the *Iliad*, Shakespeare in *Troilus and Cressida* chooses not to mention the wedding feast associated with the Apple of Discord.[11] It is incumbent upon the audience, therefore, to bring to the play the mythic material. Let me review the generally accepted facts.

During the feast to celebrate the marriage between Thetis and Peleus, King of Thessaly, all the gods and goddesses were in attendance except Eris, or Discordia, goddess of discord. Although not invited, she arrived and dropped upon the table a golden apple inscribed with the words "To the fairest." When she departed, all the goddesses claimed the apple. In the end three goddesses were left with seemingly equal claims: Juno, queen of the gods and goddess of power; Minerva, goddess of wisdom; Venus, goddess of love.[12] They decided to seek an impartial judge. This honor fell to Paris, son of Priam, king of Troy, and

Hecuba, his wife and queen. Thus each of the goddesses came to Paris, the Trojan, to convince him of her claim.

They came in turn. The first to appear to Paris was Minerva, who offered him extensive wisdom if he would but award her the prize. Next came Juno. She offered Paris unlimited power. Finally Venus appeared. She promised Paris a bride as beautiful as herself. At this Paris placed the apple in her hand. When Paris gave the apple to Venus, he offended Juno and Minerva.

We quickly translate the story of the Apple of Discord into terms that apply to *Troilus and Cressida*. Because of this contest for the Apple of Discord, the Trojans worship Venus (love) and the Greeks worship Juno (power) and Minerva (wisdom). Understanding this situation helps to make clear an essential poetic fact about the play: because the Trojans worship Venus, they have Love; because the Greeks worship Juno and Minerva, they have Power and Wisdom. The play is designed as it is in part because power and wisdom are separated from love. Generally speaking, the movement to the battlefield, therefore, is a movement toward the convergence of love with power and wisdom.

In human terms, the only real answer to the difficult circumstances of the conflict must be the fall of Troy. In thematic terms, the Trojans are and must be unsuccessful because they lack power and wisdom; the Greeks are and must be stultified because they lack love. The folly of this situation is symbolized by the two fools of the play: Pandarus, the private fool, the fool of love; Thersites, the public fool, the fool of war. So long as power and wisdom are distinct from love, there can be no concord; the continuation of the war precludes any joining of love with power and wisdom. Historically, Troy must fall in order for Rome to be founded. Thus Troy's fall is necessary because it releases the son of Venus, Aeneas, so that he may advance beyond the war and point the way to Rome, which will result in the Christian lesson of love, a higher expression of love than Troy represents.

The implications of the Apple of Discord further inform our understanding of the play. Pride and vanity are perversions of love. That the Greeks have pride is emphasized by the Prologue: "From Isles of Greece/The princes orgulous, their high blood chaf'd,/Have to the port of Athens sent their ships" (1-3). The chief exponent of pride is of course Achilles, the Greek hero. The Trojans, on the other hand, have vanity. The chief exponent of vanity is Hector, the Trojan hero. Because of the mutual separations of love from power and from wisdom, pride and vanity are pervasive sins in the play. Pride is the absence of love, and vanity is the absence of power and wisdom. Without power and wisdom, love becomes perverse. Without love, power and wisdom become perverse. Achilles won't go to war because he loves himself too much; Hector wants a trial so that he can get back what he has lost, if not to win public acclaim. As Alexander remarks, "They say [Ajax] yesterday coped Hector in the battle and struck him down, the disdain and shame whereof hath ever since kept Hector fasting and waking" (I.ii.34-37).

In terms of plot, therefore, the Trojans have what the Greeks need, Helen, Venus's gift of love. The Greeks have what the Trojans lack, power and wisdom, the favors of Juno and Minerva. Only with the fall of Troy can Helen be returned to her true husband. Thus the play concerns itself with the breakdown of the family. In Shakespeare's usual manner, the movement of the action *in a comedy* is to the establishment or the re-establishment of the family, as in *All's Well That Ends Well, Cymbeline, The Winter's Tale*. The lies that permeate the play add to this breakdown, as the entrance of Margarelon, the bastard son of Priam, demonstrates in Act V.

In this regard, therefore, the Prologue to *Troilus and Cressida* alerts us to the false and insecure nature of the world of *Troilus and Cressida*. The first sentence of the prologue, "In Troy, there lies the scene," has plurisignificance.[13] William B. Bache puts it thus:

> The first sentence of the Prologue, . . . indicates of course that the setting is to be Troy, but since we can say that the play also has the Greek camp and the field between Troy and the camp as settings, the sentence would seem to be not completely true and would seem then really to serve another purpose. Now the sentence may mean that *the scene lies in Troy* or that *the seen lies there* or, further, that *in Troy their lies are what are seen* or that *in Troy their lies are the scene*.[14]

What we see and hear in *Troilus and Cressida*, in other words, is a complex net of lies. This reality adds to the failure of Trojan society. A higher expression of love is necessary than that which Troy represents, an expression of love not infected and corrupted with lies. Thus Troy must fall. *Troilus and Cressida* brings into focus the necessity for a true expression of love, one in the context of power and wisdom.

NOTES

1. This fact is almost universally acknowledged. "The most difficult comedy

Shakespeare ever wrote" (Wolfgang Clemen, *Shakespeare's Dramatic Art* [London: Methuen, 1972], 20); "the play seems expressly to deny our wish for coherence: it will not resolve into singleness, but remains a paradox" (Jane Adamson, "Drama in the Mind: Entertaining Ideas in *Troilus and Cressida*," *The Critical Review* 27 [1985]: 6). Although I am in sympathy with her notion of the difficulty of the play, I contend that the play is coherent; we must seek our understanding from the strategies that are apparent in the play.

2. *Coleridge's Shakespeare Criticism*, ed. Thomas Middleton Raysor, 2 vols. (Cambridge: Harvard Univ. Press, 1930), 1: 109.

3. W. W. Lawrence, *Shakespeare's Problem Comedies*, 2nd ed. (New York: Fredrick Ungar Publishing Co., 1960), 3. This is the most famous and perhaps the best discussion of *Troilus and Cressida* as a "problem play." For an earlier usage of the term, however, see F. S. Boas, *Shakespeare and his Predecessors* (London: Oxford, Horace Hart, Printer to the Univ., 1896). 4. That *Troilus and Cressida* is deliberately sophisticated is maintained by Jane Adamson: "Nor does this arrive from anything inadvertent or accidental, but from what might be termed the play's deliberate recalcitrance, its aggressive unamenability" ("Drama in the Mind," 6).

5. For a discussion of the historical context of *Troilus and Cressida*, see Robert Kimbrough, *Shakespeare's Troilus and Cressida and Its Setting* (Cambridge: Harvard Univ. Press, 1964).

6. "In *Troilus and Cressida*, [Shakespeare] was dealing with one of the best known stories of his time" (Harold S. Wilson, *On the Design of Shakespearian Tragedy* [Toronto: The Univ. of Toronto Press, 1957], 116).

7. Daniel Seltzer, ed., *The History of Troilus and Cressida* in *The Complete Signet Classic Shakespeare* (New York: Harcourt Brace Jovanovich, Inc., 1963), 1002.

8. Virgil Whitaker, ed., *The History of Troilus and Cressida* (Baltimore: Penguin Books, Inc., 1970), 20.

9. Peter Alexander, *Shakespeare* (London: Oxford Univ. Press, 1964). Here Alexander discusses the special audience for which *Troilus and Cressida* first may have been performed, an audience at the Inns of Court. He posits the notion that this would have been a sophisticated group of educated men who, he implies, would have been familiar with the entire Trojan matter.

10. William B. Bache, "Affirmation in *Troilus and Cressida*," *Discourse* 10 (1967): 446-55. See also John D. Cox: "Paris' choice of Venus, in preference to Juno and Minerva, was frequently interpreted by the Elizabethans as evidence of moral myopia. . . . Though the beginning and the end of the Trojan story are not in the play, they are frequently alluded to: Troilus' story is saturated with its context, the hopeless war being waged in defense of fond Paris' original error" ("The Error of Our Eye in *Troilus and Cressida*," *Comparative Drama* 10 [1976]: 147).

11. See Margaret R. Schorer, *The Legends of Troy in Art and Literature* (New York: Phaidon Press, 1964).

12. I use the Roman names of the gods and goddesses in accordance with Shakespeare's own usage.

13. "*Troilus and Cressida* has three main locales, each of which is associated with the

main plot-line and has its own thematic environment because of the kind of action that takes place within it. . . . . The action moves through each of these locales until the three plot-lines are finally brought together and resolved in a fourth locale, the battlefield" (Kimbrough, *Shakespeare's Troilus and Cressida*, 49).

    14. See Bache, "Affirmation," 446.

2

Recapitulation in the First Two Scenes and III.i

The first several scenes of a Shakespeare play of course introduce the major characters, but they also set in motion the major concerns of a play and establish the tensions that will be explored as a play unfolds.[1] The first scenes of a play establish what I should like to call the worlds of that play.[2] For instance, the first scene of *1 Henry IV* introduces the world of Henry Bolingbroke, the present king; the second scene introduces the world of Falstaff and Hal, the subplot, if we may so put it. Hotspur is introduced in the third scene; he will become the means by which Harry will regain his lost office as the Prince of Wales. In *Hamlet* the procedure is similar: the first scene presents the midnight world of the Ghost, the former father and king; the second scene presents the world of Claudius, the new father and present king; the third scene presents the world of Polonius, the father in the subplot. In *King Lear* the first scene introduces the world of Lear, the king; the second scene introduces the world of Edmund, the principal antagonist in the subplot. Thus the first two or three scenes present and establish the major characters and the primary themes and tensions.

The first two scenes of *Troilus and Cressida* present a variant of the familiar strategy. Although the title of the play is *Troilus and Cressida*, the Prologue announces that the subject of the play is the Trojan War. But the first scene presents the Troilus world, and the second scene presents the Cressida world:

first the world of Troilus then the world of Cressida, as the title would suggest. The relationship of Troilus and Cressida to the main subject matter, therefore, is strangely and immediately insisted upon. The play begins with what, in terms of the Prologue, is the subplot and with what, in terms of the title, is the main plot. In the difficult *Troilus and Cressida*, Shakespeare seems to insist on the primary importance of both the public plot, which as the Prologue indicates involves Paris and Helen, and the private plot, which as the title suggests involves Troilus and Cressida.[3] We may well suppose that each plot will become a version of the other: Cressida, for instance, is a localized and unmarried Helen.

In any event, Shakespeare seems intent on making clear the nature of each world, of each of the scenes, by providing the scenes with comparable features. For instance, each scene contains a soliloquy, one by Troilus and one by Cressida, a feature that we might expect in a scene that emphasizes a major character. Pandarus appears first with Troilus and then with Cressida. Each scene uses a significant sound: the first scene presents alarms; the second scene presents a retreat. Moreover, in the first scene Troilus and Pandarus discuss a process, the baking of bread; in the second scene Cressida and Pandarus discuss a procession, the returning soldiers. But the main point is that we are given the private worlds of Troilus and Cressida before any public world is emphasized.

Although there are important similarities between the first two scenes of *Troilus and Cressida*, there are also important differences. For example, Troilus's soliloquy in the first scene reveals his importunity to achieve Cressida; Cressida's soliloquy in the second scene reveals her intent not to surrender to that importunity, as conveyed to her by Pandarus. Each soliloquy is part of the plot action, although the view we get of Cressida here is surprising in light of how quickly she later surrenders. Moreover, although Pandarus tells Troilus that he doesn't like wooing Cressida on Troilus's behalf, he then tells Cressida that Troilus is better than the other Trojans. The alarms we hear in the first scene signify the beginning of the day's conflict; the retreat we hear in the second scene signifies the end of the day's conflict. In the course of the first two scenes, therefore, a single day passes in which against the background of the public dispute we see the play's private problem, the developing relationship between Troilus and Cressida. In terms of design, the discussion of the process of baking bread in the first scene is balanced by the procession of soldiers in the second scene. The process seems to be a trope for the Troilus world; the procession seems to be a trope for the Cressida world. We may suppose that this process qualifies the action of the play in Troilus's terms; this procession expresses the nature of the play in Cressida's terms; that is, both the process and the procession are tropes that are to be used as means by which to understand the action in terms of Troilus and Cressida.

That the play begins with Troilus and Cressida is important, although, considering the title of the play, not surprising. That each of the first two scenes contains a soliloquy by the major character in the scene is significant. For what Shakespeare is doing is presenting, first, the essential Troilus problem and, second, the essential Cressida problem. Shakespeare often seems to want to give us an essential scene in terms of an important character as quickly as he can. In *1 Henry IV*, for instance, Hal has a soliloquy in the second scene, the scene in which Shakespeare presents the essential Hal, the calculating prince: we are introduced to a young man sick of play and idleness. In the second scene of *Hamlet*, Hamlet delivers a soliloquy in which we hear a melancholy young man who is contemplating suicide. In the second scene of *King Lear*, Edmund's three soliloquies reveal the calculating bastard son. In each case we are shown a young, discontented man: Hal, Hamlet, Edmund, Troilus. In each instance Shakespeare includes a soliloquy in an early, crucial scene, one that establishes a central character, a crucial young man who will determine in large part the subsequent action. In the first Act Shakespeare presents an unhappy, young man, who will be of vital importance at and by the end of the play.

One difference between these other plays and *Troilus and Cressida* is that only in the problem play does the heroine have a soliloquy. Another difference is that Troilus and Cressida and their soliloquies are presented immediately, not, as in the other plays, after the initial situation has been established in the first scene. One reason for this difference is that in *Troilus and Cressida* the initial emphasis is on the private action, rather than on the public action, as in *1 Henry IV*, *Hamlet*, and *King Lear*. After the first alarm, Troilus speaks:

> Peace, you ungracious clamours! Peace, rude sounds!
> Fools on both sides, Helen must needs be fair
> When with your blood you daily paint her thus.
> I cannot fight upon this argument;
> It is too starv'd a subject for my sword.
> But Pandarus—O gods, how do you plague me!
> I cannot come to Cressid but by Pandar,
> And he's as tetchy to be woo'd to woo
> As she is stubborn-chaste against all suit.
> Tell me, Apollo, for thy Daphne's love,
> What Cressid is, what Pandar, and what we.
> Her bed is India; there she lies, a pearl.

> Between our Ilium and where she resides,
> Let it be call'd the wild and wand'ring flood,
> Ourself the merchant, and this sailing Pandar
> Our doubtful hope, our convoy and our bark.
>
> (I.i.89-104)

Like Hal, Hamlet, and Edmund—Shakespeare's other young men with soliloquies—Troilus is depicted here as a troubled young man.[4] In this case, Troilus's trouble stems from his preoccupation with Cressida. He knows that Pandarus is the bark that will carry him to her. For Troilus as lover, Pandarus has a significant role. But as Pandarus remarks, "I will leave all as I found it, and there an end" (I.i.87-88). By the end of the play Troilus's position will be not a lover but a revenger. He will reject Cressida and pursue the war. Thus Troilus will no longer need Pandarus. No marriage will take place. At the outset Pandarus is entrusted by an importunate prince to bring him to Cressida; at the end of the play, when the private and the public worlds have joined on the battlefield, all three will have been badly damaged. But then Pandarus, the instrument of love, acknowledges the truth: "Why should our endeavour be so loved and the performance so loathed?" (V.x.38-40)

The second scene naturally follows the first in that Pandarus has now come to Cressida on Troilus's behalf. Thus the second scene is directly comparable to the first. As I have indicated, the major character delivers a soliloquy. I should like to suggest that the first scene establishes two Troilus's, or a Troilus with a dual role: the love-sick boy of the soliloquy, who wants to unarm for love; the armed soldier of the end of the scene, who goes off with Aeneas to battle. Similarly, in the second scene there are two Cressida's. In her interchange with Pandarus, Cressida claims to have no interest in Troilus, yet in her soliloquy, which ends the scene, she reveals her desire for the young prince.[5] As a means of preserving herself, Cressida vows not to submit to Troilus:

> Words, vows, gifts, tears, and love's full sacrifice
> He offers in another's enterprise;
> But more in Troilus thousand-fold I see
> Than in the glass of Pandar's praise may be;
> Yet hold I off. Women are angels wooing:
> Things won are done; joy's soul lies in the doing.
> That she belov'd knows naught that knows not this:
> Men prize the thing ungain'd more than it is.
> That she was never yet that ever knew

> Love got so sweet as when desire did sue.
> Therefore this maxim out of love I teach:
> 'Achievement is command; ungain'd, beseech.'
> Then though my heart's content firm love doth bear,
> Nothing of that shall from mine eyes appear.
>
> (I.ii.287-300)

Again, the reason Shakespeare creates two scenes so obviously similar is that he is providing a version of the action of the play first in Troilus's terms and then in Cressida's terms. For example, the first scene has three stages: Troilus and Pandarus; Troilus alone; Troilus and Aeneas. And the scene has "rude sounds" (I.i.89), specifically the sounding of the alarm. It is sounded twice, once before the soliloquy and once after the soliloquy: alarms bracket the soliloquy, emphasizing its significance. In effect, it is the sound of the alarm that signifies the exit of Pandarus and the entrance of Aeneas. Pandarus is on one side of the Troilus soliloquy; Aeneas is on the other. We may further say that the alarm calls our attention to Pandarus's exit and to Aeneas's entrance. Pandarus leaves; the essential Troilus speaks; Aeneas enters. Pandarus is asked to play Cupid, the son of Venus; Aeneas is the true son of Venus.

The Prologue identifies the "quarrel":

> From Isles of Greece
> The princes orgulous, their high blood chaf'd,
> Have to the port of Athens sent their ships
> Fraught with the ministers and instruments
> Of cruel war: sixty and nine that wore
> Their crownets regal, from th'Athenian bay
> Put forth toward Phrygia, and their vow is made
> To ransack Troy, within whose strong immures
> The ravish'd Helen, Menelaus' queen,
> With wanton Paris sleeps—and that's the quarrel.
>
> (1-10)

It seems surprising that, in a play identifying the relationship between Paris and Helen as the source or the cause of the Greek invasion of Troy, Helen should appear on stage only once, in III.i. In that scene she is referred to as the "mortal Venus" (III.i.31). Also in III.i Cressida and Helen are identified. Pandarus, in response to the servant's reference to the "mortal Venus," asks, "Who, my cousin Cressida?" (III.i.33) The point is that Venus is a goddess; Helen is half a goddess; Cressida is only mortal. Helen is married, and the "quarrel" is to get Helen back to her husband. Cressida isn't married. Her hope for a viable future is invested in a frail uncle and a frail lover; part of Troilus's problem is, as he indicates, that he is "weaker than a woman's tear" (I.i.9). The implications are clear. In his attempt to have Cressida, Troilus wants to do what Paris did. The Apple of Discord qualifies this identification. That Troilus would achieve Cressida is, in human terms, as damaging as Paris's achievement of Helen. In symbolic terms, love, whether in the form of Helen or Cressida, has become a commodity.

Aeneas is the son of Venus. In terms of the design of the play's first scene, Aeneas replaces Pandarus. Generally speaking, the structure of the first scene resembles the structure of the Troilus action in the play. Troilus begins the first scene with Pandarus; Troilus ends this scene with Aeneas. Similarly, Troilus begins the play with Pandarus; Troilus ends the play with Aeneas. In IV.ii Aeneas comes to escort Cressida to the Greek camp in exchange for Antenor:

> *Cressida.* Did I not tell you? Would he were knock'd i'th'
> head!   *One knocks*
>   (IV.ii.34-35)

After some discussion, Aeneas enters, effectively replacing Pandarus in the Troilus action. Here in IV.ii Aeneas has the responsibility of taking Cressida to the Greeks; the knocking upon which Aeneas enters in IV.ii reminds us of the alarm upon which he enters in the play's first scene. In IV.ii Aeneas comes to take Cressida away; in the play's first scene Aeneas comes to take Troilus away. The point is that the first scene is charged with meaning by the subsequent action of the play.[6] We do not see the meaning implicit in I.i, however, until we refer the rest of the play to it.

In addition, the play begins and ends with these three characters: Pandarus, Troilus, and Aeneas appear both in the first scene and in V.x, the last scene of the play. Not only is Aeneas the son of Venus but also Pandarus is put into the Cupid role by the action of Calchas, Cressida's treacherous father, by Troilus, the besotted lover, and by Cressida, Pandarus's willing niece. In III.i, the Helen-Paris-Pandarus scene (the only scene in which Helen appears in the play), Helen describes and thus establishes Pandarus as a kind of Cupid. Pandarus's song, therefore, is vital and serves a choric function much as a soliloquy does. Pandarus's choric instrument is then not dissimilar to the soliloquies of I.i, Troilus's scene, and I.ii, Cressida's scene:[7]

Love, love, nothing but love, still love, still more!
For O love's bow
Shoots buck and doe;
The shaft confounds
Not that it wounds,
But tickles still the sore.
These lovers cry O ho, they die!
Yet that which seems the wound to kill
Doth turn O ho, to Ha, ha, he!
So dying love lives still.
O ho, a while, but Ha, ha, ha!
O ho, groans out for Ha, ha, ha!—Heigh ho!
(III.i.110-21)

This song is qualified in the light of the Apple of Discord. Love here is only Cupid love; it has no power and wisdom. When Cressida is delivered to the Greeks, love in the form of Cressida engages power and wisdom, but as Cressida's soliloquy demonstrates, her love (once given) is devalued. As she correctly indicates, "Achievement is command; ungain'd, beseech" (I.ii.298). By such assessment, we see how sodden the relationship between Paris and Helen is. In terms of structure, III.i serves as a prologue or an introduction to the first meeting between Troilus and Cressida, which occurs in III.ii. It alerts us to the basis of the relationship between Troilus and Cressida.

What seems to be serving only a plot function is serving a deeper purpose: the soliloquies of the first two scenes and the song of III.i serve as a digested or condensed version of the action of *Troilus and Cressida*, a digestion also of the epic material, as the Prologue indicates. I do not think that we see at once the recapitulative nature of these scenes. As I have indicated, they are charged with meaning after the fact. Yet as a strategy, recapitulation helps to make clear the essential action of several characters. For example, Troilus begins the scene and the play by resolving not to fight: "Call here my varlet, I'll unarm again./Why should I war without the walls of Troy,/That find such cruel battle here within?" (I.i.1-3) He ends the scene by going with Aeneas off to battle, as we have seen:

> *Aeneas.* Hark what good sport is out of town today.
> *Troilus.* Better at home, if 'would I might' were 'may'.
> But to the sport abroad—are you bound thither?

Aeneas. In all swift haste.

Troilus.   Come, go we then together.

(I.i.113-17)

Although Troilus does not have his heart in the public cause, he goes off to fight. By the end of the play, he has discarded his heart, and the only cause he has is that of revenge. The first scene condenses and digests Troilus's action in the entire play by reflecting his movement from the sentimental love-sick boy in the first scene of the play to the hardened soldier in the last scene of the play. As we learn at the end of I.ii, Cressida wants Troilus. All Pandarus does is to supply the gear, as he indicates he has done at the end of III.ii. When Troilus lets Cressida go to the Greek camp, he isolates himself. In structural terms, Troilus's isolation in the middle of the play is reflected by his soliloquy in the middle of the first scene. Pandarus is with him before the soliloquy; Aeneas is with him after the soliloquy. Similarly, Pandarus brings Troilus to Cressida; Aeneas follows Cressida, as we see when Aeneas comes to fetch Cressida in the fourth Act and when he accompanies Troilus on the battlefield in Act V. In the private action of the play, what Troilus believes to be an avenue to Cressida becomes a way to isolation. By both the end of the first scene and the end of the play Troilus feels that he must fight.[8] He will go about the battlefield in Act V in search of Diomedes. His "sport" will be to kill Diomedes.

Given the nature of the play's first scene, we expect in the second scene to get the action of the play from Cressida's perspective. And, like Troilus's soliloquy in I.i, Cressida's soliloquy in I.ii is of vital importance: it presents the essential Cressida. The speech begins with a list, which is not unexpected, for after a procession, a list, a procession of words, seems natural: "Words, vows, gifts, tears, and love's full sacrifice" (I.ii.287). This list provides a version of the Cressida movement in the play. Cressida's position at the outset of the play is on the level of words: she tells Pandarus that she is not interested in Troilus. She asserts that she will hold off her affection for Troilus, but she actually capitulates to him in her next scene, III.ii. There Cressida decides not to adhere to her private vow. It is not surprising, then, that she encounters difficulties.

The list is one in a series of strategies, therefore, that enables Shakespeare to deliver the material to us in a condensed, sophisticated manner. In the first scene the major trope is the process of baking bread. In the second scene the major trope is the procession of soldiers. The process in the first scene may be applied to the Troilus action: Pandarus advises him to be patient, yet he is too importunate; he should not act until the bread is baked and ready to eat. Cressida, on the other hand, watches the procession of Trojan soldiers in the second scene.

The procession will be re-introduced in IV.v when, in a version of the procedure in I.ii, she confronts a procession of Greek soldiers. Thus the process, the procession, and the list seem to be versions of comparable strategies.

Because we know the full story, we can see how Cressida might have averted difficulty. One solution might have been to keep her word and not to submit to Troilus. Another solution might have been marriage, a Shakespearean symbol for unity, for had Cressida not given in to Troilus before they were married, Troilus might have acted differently: he could have acknowledged his wife, but, as we know, he is infected with the Trojan sin of vanity; he has neither power nor wisdom. Of course Cressida is trapped by her clandestine relationship with Troilus and does not wish to be exposed publicly either. For after Cressida commits to Troilus in III.ii she is no longer free. As she says in her soliloquy,

> Women are angels, wooing:
> Things won are done; joy's soul lies in the doing.
> That she belov'd knows naught that knows not this:
> Men prize the thing ungain'd more than it is.
>
> (I.ii.291-94)

Part, then, of the Cressida problem is timing: had she not given herself to Troilus when she did, tragedy might have been averted. Again, the Apple of Discord informs our understanding. Cressida and Troilus behave as they do because all they have is love; they have neither power nor wisdom, and because they lack power and wisdom this "affair" is the result. We may be meant to intuit the offstage pressure that leads her to capitulate to Troilus, but since Cressida acknowledges that she loves him and that she has no one to support her, she is ready (whether she knows it or not) to capitulate. As she says in III.ii, "Hard to seem won; but I was won, my lord,/With the first glance" (III.ii.116-17).

Yet Cressida's action in the play moves from words through vows, gifts, tears, to love's full sacrifice—terms that chart, in at least a general way, Cressida's movement through the five Acts of the play. For her position at the end of the play is a difficult one: Cressida is the daughter of Calchas, who has betrayed Troy; she is delivered to the Greeks by Troilus; she has lost her lover, Troilus, who along with Aeneas delivers her to Diomedes; she must do what she can to preserve herself. This is not to say that she is blameless, for with Pandarus, Troilus, and her father, Calchas, she bears a share of the responsibility for her fate. In recapitulative terms, however, the soliloquy comes at the end of the second scene as a means of indicating Cressida's position at the end of the play: alone, isolated, separated from everything she loves. Troilus ends the play with

Pandarus and Aeneas. Like the first scene with the emphasis on the Troilus action, the design of the second scene is a digestion or condensation of the Cressida action in the play. Troilus is alone in the middle of the first scene in a reflection of his isolation in the middle of the action of the play. Once Cressida is given over to the Greeks, Troilus feels alone and betrayed; by V.x, however, he again meets Pandarus and Aeneas. Cressida, on the other hand, ends the second scene alone and speaking a soliloquy, a structural device that reflects her isolation at the end of the play. In terms of the list at the beginning of Cressida's speech, we are admonished to see that Cressida ends as "love's full sacrifice."[9] Troilus doesn't hear this soliloquy, and he doesn't see or hear her grief in Act IV. From Troilus's singular perspective, Cressida is only words, "no matter from the heart" (V.iii.108); from her point-of-view, she has suffered the full sacrifice of heart-felt love. We are informed by our understanding of the implications of the Apple of Discord and by the entire dramatic construct of the play: Cressida, the Trojan girl, represents love, a diminished, undervalued love, love bereft of wisdom and power. Her frail "husband" abandons her; her brutal "lover" uses her.

Another function of the soliloquy is that it invites us to re-think the action of the scene and to consider Cressida's behavior later in the play. That it ends the scene is important because Shakespeare appears to be counting on our recognition of the recapitulative design of the scene, although, again, I don't think we recognize this until we are quite familiar with the play. The scene is charged with meaning by subsequent action. For unlike Troilus who depends upon Pandarus, Cressida asserts that she does not need Pandarus's prodding: "But more in Troilus thousand-fold I see/Than in the glass of Pandar's praise may be" (I.ii.289-90). Still, Pandarus has been performing the role of surrogate father. For, as we have seen, the family is an essential Shakespeare trope, and in *Troilus and Cressida* the fractured family is a crucial issue in the play. Just as Cressida is eventually kept from Troilus, so the war is keeping Helen from Menelaus. Yet Pandarus is not a real father, and Cressida has seemingly resisted Pandarus's efforts to procure her favor for Troilus. Her essential position is here revealed; in her speech she tells us the truth about her feelings. All has been show, as she tells Troilus in III.ii. Pandarus has been duped. Her rhetoric throughout the scene is qualified by her soliloquy at the end of the scene. The logic of her behavior, she believes, has been sound: "Men prize the thing ungain'd more than it is" (I.ii.294). The fact is that Cressida doesn't need Pandarus's persuasion, nor really does Troilus, although he thinks he does. Nevertheless, Pandarus does go to Helen in III.i, and he provides the "gear" for Troilus and Cressida in III.ii. Still Troilus and Cressida are destroyed, as it were, because they employ and rely on

Pandarus or Cupid, as Helen calls him, for in III.ii Troilus and Cressida allow Pandarus to bring them together. Cressida, therefore, does not adhere to what she tells herself here in the play's second scene. Thus we get Cressida's "philosophy" in the soliloquy, the essential girl, as Shakespeare employs a strategy similar to that which he employs in *1 Henry IV*, *Hamlet*, and *King Lear*. The difference here is that Cressida has replaced the young hero of those plays.

By delivering her maxim, Cressida extends her philosophy. It is the only instance in the canon that Shakespeare employs this term: "this maxim out of love I teach:/'Achievement is command; ungain'd, beseech'" (I.ii, 297-98). It is her greatest truth, the speech, as maxim, that carries the most weight. That it is spoken "out of love" is significant. On the one hand, we can read this as a proverbial speech whose subject is the nature of love; it explains Cressida's understanding of love and its implications. On the other hand, "out of love" can be read as outside of love. "Achievement" and "command" are words more normally associated with battle than with love. Although employed by Cressida, the terms are applicable to warfare. This maxim invokes love and violence, or, more exactly, lust and violence. With Pandarus she has just watched soldiers return from battle. In effect, war is associated with love, and love with war. Shakespeare is brutally clear about the nature of both. And as we witness in the play, Troilus and Cressida become sacrifices to the violence of unregulated love and war.

Further, as a feature of the recapitulative scene, the soliloquy must be applied to an understanding of Cressida's action in the rest of the play. Once Cressida does not keep her word not to capitulate to Troilus, she has lost her value, as she acknowledges. Immediately after III.ii, Cressida is considered a commodity, an object for the trade.[10] Ulysses dubs her one of the "daughters of the game" (IV.v.63). Gain and loss, as implied by her maxim, is the nature of her situation. When in IV.v she is kissed by the Greeks in a kind of procession, she is but an object, something to be won or lost. Although she can refuse Menelaus, she cannot ignore the Greeks; she has no position. A prisoner has little privilege. Moreover, in V.ii, the crucial scene in which, cloaked in shadows, Troilus and Ulysses watch Cressida and Diomedes, Cressida's position is equally as desperate. She cannot refuse Diomedes. She has been gained by the Greeks: "Achievement" has become "command." Love has gone over to the Greeks, but to no good end, for love is made subservient to power, and wisdom is not effective.

NOTES

1. I am greatly indebted to William B. Bache for the critical term recapitulation, which appears in the title of this chapter and throughout the book. See *Design and Closure in Shakespeare's Major Plays: The Nature of Recapitulation* (New York: Peter Lang, 1991).

2. See G. Wilson Knight, *The Wheel of Fire* (1949; rpt. London: Methuen, 1970). Knight discusses the two sides of the conflict as the opposition between beauty and worth and the bestial elements in man.

3. See D.A. Traversi, *An Approach to Shakespeare*, rev.ed. (Garden City: Doubleday, 1969), 2: 3.

4. Angela Pitt, *Shakespeare's Women* (London: David H. Charles, 1981). Ms. Pitt discusses Troilus's troubles in terms of his sexual indulgence.

5. Troilus and Cressida "could hardly be worse matched. He is all words and passion; she all ivory and calculation" (Robert Kimbrough, *Shakespeare's Troilus and Cressida and Its Setting* [Cambridge: Harvard Univ. Press, 1964], 79).

6. See Bache, *Design and Closure*, 58. Bache discusses this procedure in terms of *As You Like It*.

7. Generally speaking, the design of III.i is like the design of I.i and I.ii. Each scene begins with two characters on stage. They are joined by a character or characters. Act I.i begins with Troilus and Pandarus; Aeneas enters the scene later. Act I.ii begins with Cressida and Alexander; Pandarus then joins them on stage. Act III.i begins with Pandarus and a nameless servant; they are joined by Paris and Helen. There are, of course, differences, but the general strategy seems to be the same.

8. Alexander's account of Hector in I.ii is designed to show us Hector's vanity: he is after a public image. And Hector and Troilus seem meant to be equated. It is a commonplace that Troilus will become like Hector after the great warrior's death. Troilus's desire for battle in the last act of the play is made clear: it too is an act of vanity.

9. For a representative sample of anti-Cressida comment see the following: Una Ellis-Fermor, *The Frontiers of Drama* (London: Methuen, 1964); Mary Ellen Rickey, "'Twixt the Dangerous Shores': *Troilus and Cressida* Again," *Shakespeare Quarterly* 15 (1964): 3-13; L. C. Knights, *Some Shakespearean Themes* (London: Chatto and Windus, 1959); William W. Lawrence, *Shakespeare's Problem Comedies* (New York: Fredrick Ungar, 1960). John Cox notes that "Cressida is, in fact, Shakespeare's only faithless heroine, a point that makes her play anomalous yet provides a touchstone by default for comparison with other plays" ("The Error in Our Eye in *Troilus and Cressida*," *Comparative Drama* 10 [1976]: 147). Although Cox's observation is correct, his conclusion cries for comment. That Cressida is perceived as faithless is all the more questionable in the light of how Shakespeare treats his other heroines. The point is that Cressida, like the other women in Shakespeare's plays, is not so faithless as she is a sacrifice to love and war. Carolyn Asp also comes to Cressida's defense: "Cressida is left to the mercies of those who will use her to satisfy their immediate needs" ("In Defense of Cressida," *Studies in Philology* 74 [1977]: 417).

10. Once Cressida surrenders herself, she becomes a commodity. This word is used in

the 1609 quarto, in the Epistle to the reader, in *King John*, and at the end of III.iii in *Much Ado About Nothing*. In the Epistle to the reader commodity is used as a pun with comedy. The point is that in *Troilus and Cressida* people are used, as if they are commodities, things meant to be used. Cressida is used in the trade; Troilus's initial attitude toward Cressida is depicted in the imagery of eating, as if to Troilus Cressida is as kind of dish meant to be eaten and digested.

3

Character and Theme in the First Five Scenes

One of the remarkable features of *Troilus and Cressida* is the strangeness of its beginning: a prologue followed by five scenes that do not emphasize plot development. Kenneth Muir, one of the most respected of Shakespeare critics, makes the following observation:

> *Troilus and Cressida*, indeed, is unique even among Shakespeare's works in its changes of viewpoint from scene to scene. In the first scene, for example, every reader and every member of an audience looks at the situation through the eyes of Troilus, in the second through the eyes of Cressida, in the third through the eyes of Ulysses, in the fourth through the eyes of Thersites, and in the fifth through the eyes of Hector.[1]

Muir's insight is valuable and, with some qualification, can be usefully applied. For Muir's notion that the first five scenes of *Troilus and Cressida* provide five different points of view is not completely accurate. To this notion we must add that what Shakespeare does in the first five scenes is to introduce characters and to present themes. Just as the prologue is a point of reference for us as we proceed through the play, so the first five scenes perform a comparable but much more elaborate function. We come back to and draw upon the first five scenes as we proceed through the rest of the play. But, again, if we examine the first five scenes in the light of the Muir insight we can see how serviceable and useful it is.

As we noted in the preceding chapter, Shakespeare traditionally introduces all of the major characters at the beginning of a play, and he usually uses separate scenes in order to do this. As we indicated, in *1 Henry IV*, *Hamlet*, and *King Lear* the major characters are introduced and established at once: we may say that the essential worlds of the play are presented with cogency and precision at once. The first scene of *1 Henry IV* presents Henry Bolingbroke, the present king; the second scene introduces Falstaff and Hal, the major characters in what at this juncture may be called the subplot; the third scene introduces Hotspur, the means by which Prince Harry will regain his lost office as the Prince of Wales, as he moves toward being Henry V. The first scene of *Hamlet* presents the ghost, the aged father and past king; the second scene introduces Claudius, the uncle-father and present king, and Hamlet; and the third scene documents the world of Polonius, the father, Ophelia and Laertes. The first scene of *King Lear* introduces Lear, the king; the second scene documents the subplot world of Edmund, the bastard son, Edgar and Gloucester. It is striking to note that the young hero—Prince Harry, Hamlet, Edgar—is introduced in the second scene of each play. This hero will rise to public prominence as the play draws to its close.

In *Troilus and Cressida* the procedure is different. For one thing, the play, like *Romeo and Juliet* and *Antony and Cleopatra*, has two titular characters.[2] The first scene introduces Troilus; the second scene introduces Cressida. As I have demonstrated, we get not just their two perspectives or their two viewpoints but two recapitulations of the action: first Troilus's, then Cressida's. Muir's term, *viewpoint*, is useful but not so precise as the term *recapitulation*, for, although each viewpoint is presented, the term does not allow for the careful and deliberate design of these scenes. As everyone acknowledges, the play has both a private plot and a public plot. And Shakespeare wants to establish the complementary worlds of the two lovers before proceeding to the public plot. Again, the first two scenes concern Troilus and Cressida, the private plot. Part of the reason for this reversal (the young hero being introduced at once) concerns, in part, the different "tone" of *Troilus and Cressida*, which emphasizes the private rather than the public plot.

The emphasis in the first two scenes, however, is on love and war, the main subject of the play. But, more important, the emphasis on love is an oblique emphasis on the trope of the Apple of Discord. Now it is true that I.iii, the Greek council scene, and II.i, the Ajax-Thersites-Achilles-Patroclus scene, and II.ii, the

Trojan council scene, do serve to introduce new characters, both Greeks and Trojans. But the main point is that these three scenes concern the public plot. We, further, see that the Muir point about the viewpoint in these three scenes needs severe modification. To make the point more exactly: as applied, the trope of the Apple of Discord determines that Troilus and Cressida have only love: they have no power and wisdom. Act I.iii presents the world of the Greeks in terms of a public debate on whether or not to continue the war. Thus Muir's insight needs to be not just qualified, but refined. Troilus is on stage throughout the first scene; Cressida is on stage throughout the second scene. If, as I should like to argue, one rule of the recapitulative scene is that a character must be on stage throughout that scene, then the next three scenes do not, strictly speaking, observe the rule: in I.iii Ulysses and Nestor are on stage throughout the scene; in II.i no one is on stage throughout the scene; in II.ii all of the Trojans are on stage throughout the scene. There is no single viewpoint in any of these three scenes. But it is interesting to note that none of the Greeks in I.iii, the Greek council, is in the Greek II.i.

In *1 Henry IV*, *Hamlet*, and *King Lear*, Shakespeare employs only two or three scenes to establish the worlds of the major characters, but in *Troilus and Cressida* he may be said to use five scenes. The size and complexity of the subject matter would seem to determine, as I have argued, a more elaborate procedure than in these other plays. As the Prologue indicates, a digestion of the epic material will be presented: "what may be digested in a play" (29). In the first five scenes then the major characters are introduced and the worlds they inhabit are documented.

After Shakespeare recapitulates the action of the play from the perspectives of Troilus in the first scene and Cressida in the second, the plot emphasis shifts with I.iii: in this and the following two scenes the specific subject will be the war and its continuance. Ulysses, Achilles, Ajax, and Hector are established as the major figures of the public plot. First Ulysses commands the stage in I.iii with his speech on degree, establishing his version of the cause of the Greek failure to end the war quickly.[3] As the Greek leaders debate the lack of success, Ulysses seizes the opportunity to blame their failure on not observing degree and order.[4] But what he really wants to do is to subvert degree and order, to undercut Agamemnon. Instead of wanting to encourage Achilles to fight, he wants to prevent Achilles from fighting. Like Hector in II.ii, whom we have heard about in I.ii as having issued a proclamation because he was defeated by Ajax, Ulysses is being political. He wishes to gain control by promoting Ajax at the expense of Achilles: he wants to bring Achilles, the great Greek warrior, down. In the first scene of Act II, we see the effect of the proclamation on the two principal subjects, Achilles and Ajax. In II.i Achilles expects to be regarded as Hector's equal in battle. Achilles, therefore, is the Greek equivalent of the Trojan Hector. In I.ii we learn that Hector is upset because Ajax defeated him. In II.ii Hector, having been defeated by Ajax, wants to redeem himself by meeting and defeating Achilles. Act II.i concerns the proclamation that is the product of I.iii. The scene concerns Achilles and Ajax, the warriors not present in I.iii. The main point is that Ulysses succeeds in keeping Achilles in his tent; then in II.ii Hector does what he can to get Achilles out of his tent. But we know that Ulysses has already won. If Hector fights anyone it will have to be Ajax. We will see what the effect of that confrontation is in IV.v, when Hector and Ajax meet.

Hector clearly becomes the dominant figure in the Trojan council of II.ii by first winning the debate with Paris and Troilus and then capitulating to what he has demonstrated by his argument is an unwarranted position.[5] Act II.ii presents the Trojans in debate over the question of the continuance of the war. Hector demonstrates that the war cannot be defended. But then he votes to continue the war. The public Hector proves his acumen and then submits to the discredited Paris and Troilus. Like Ulysses in the Greek council of I.iii, who subverts equality and has his way, Hector performs a comparable action in II.ii. Thus I.iii and II.ii are complementary.

In the Greek council of I.iii, the Achilles scene of II.i, and the Trojan council of II.ii we are given the public plot. Act II.i introduces Thersites, who corresponds to Pandarus in the private plot: one is the fool of the Trojan world; the other is the fool of the Greek world. In terms of the Apple of Discord, I.iii, the Greek council, presents wisdom without power or love; II.i, the Achilles scene, presents power without wisdom or love; II.ii, the Trojan council, presents love without wisdom or power. This is one reason for two Greek scenes and one Trojan scene. We see what happens to wisdom without love in I.iii, the Greek council; we see what happens to power without love in II.i, the Achilles scene; we see what happens to love without wisdom and power in II.ii, the Trojan council. Shakespeare is not so much interested in character recapitulation in these three scenes, I.iii, II.i, II.ii. To put it succinctly, in the first two scenes of the play the emphasis is on character; in the next three scenes the emphasis is on theme. The first two scenes establish the two titular characters; the next three scenes emphasize theme.

The Greek and Trojan council scenes, I.iii and II.ii, have long been regarded as structural peculiarities of the play.[6] To critics and scholars the scenes are generally considered clumsy, long, and intellectual.[7] Why Shakespeare would wish to include two scenes so seemingly uncharacteristic is a question whose answer partially is to be found in the Muir formulation.[8] Act I.iii presents more than the Ulysses viewpoint, however: it provides the public world of the Greeks, the political debate, and wisdom perverted by the action of Ulysses and, to a lesser extent, Nestor. Act II.ii presents more than the Hector viewpoint; it presents the public world of the Trojans, the debate in the Trojan council, and love perverted by Paris, Troilus, and Hector. The Greek council scene, I.iii, contains Agamemnon, Nestor, Ulysses, Diomedes, Menelaus—all Greek leaders—with Ulysses delivering his famous, rhetorical speech on order and degree; yet Ulysses, as I have noted, is interested in only power: he doesn't care who nominally rules; he wants to control, as the end of the scene makes clear, and he does gain control. On the other hand, the Trojan council scene, II.ii, contains Priam, Hector, Troilus, Paris, Helenus in debate over keeping Helen, thus prolonging the war. Hector, like Ulysses, prevails in the scene, gaining control in the course of the debate. Both Ulysses and Hector seem to argue for the general good; both end up by serving themselves.[9] Thus these scenes appear to mirror each other.[10] The design of each scene reveals a striking similarity to that of the other scene. Thus the scenes may be said to be complementary.[11] The recapitulative nature of I.i and I.ii—the Troilus and Cressida scenes—encourages us to see I.iii and II.ii as recapitulations of the Greek and Trojan action in the play. Following the private view of Troilus and Cressida, Shakespeare presents in I.iii and II.ii the public view of the Greeks and the Trojans, two scenes that make clear the thematic implications of the Apple of Discord. We see in I.iii how disastrous wisdom is without love; we see in II.ii how disastrous love is without wisdom and power.

Both I.iii and II.ii begin with five named characters. Agamemnon's speech begins I.iii; Priam's speech begins II.ii. Ulysses's speech on degree "becomes," in a manner of speaking, Troilus's speech on will and judgment. The only new person to enter I.iii is Aeneas; the only new person to enter II.ii is Cassandra. Granted the thematic thrust of the Apple of Discord, we may suppose that in I.iii, the Greek council scene, Aeneas comes on stage as the symbolic answer to the Greek problem, for he is the son of Venus, the symbolic representative of love, the Trojan virtue that the Greeks lack. Cassandra, on the other hand, seems to represent the wisdom that the Trojans lack. Love is needed in the Greek I.iii; wisdom is needed in the Trojan II.ii. Cassandra is wise but ignored and disregarded. The little debate between Troilus and Helenus, which, on the surface, doesn't seem to be significant, is thematically important. For Helenus is meant to be seen as power, a special kind of power, the power of faith. Helenus, the priest who represents the special power of faith, is dismissed by Troilus with "You are for dreams and slumbers, brother priest" (II.ii.37). Just as Aeneas makes no difference in I.iii, the Greek council, so Cassandra and Helenus make no difference in II.ii, the Trojan council.

We may equate Agamemnon with Priam, Aeneas with Cassandra, Ulysses with Hector. In the Greek council scene, I.iii, Ulysses pays lip service to degree and then undermines it by conspiring with Nestor; in the Trojan council scene, II.ii, Hector pays lip service to the madness of continuing the war and then undermines it by agreeing with Paris and Troilus that the war should continue. By entering the Greek camp with a challenge, Aeneas provides an opportunity *for* Ulysses. Hector reveals his challenge after Cassandra enters II.ii. Ulysses uses Aeneas; Hector disregards Cassandra. Thus both Ulysses and Hector sacrifice the public good to a private cause. Aeneas in I.iii is balanced in II.ii by first Helenus, power, and then by Cassandra, wisdom, first power and then wisdom. In this way these scenes fill out each other and present the thematic and trenchant implications of the Apple of Discord trope.

Aeneas is not in II.i because he is not involved in the Achilles-Ajax-Thersites subplot. He is not in II.ii because he is not involved in the public Trojan debate about the war: he is at the service of Hector. Love comes to the Greek camp with Cressida and Hector in IV.v, but they are both accommodated with disastrous results. Love will have an effect in the Greek world when Achilles receives the letter from Queen Hecuba. Yet Aeneas is involved with the Troilus and Hector action: he appears in I.i and I.iii. As we have seen, Aeneas, the son of Venus, will replace Pandarus, the fool of love, when Pandarus is "knock'd i'th'head" (34-35) in IV.ii. Aeneas is involved in the private plot; in IV.iv he will come to accompany Cressida to the Greek camp.

The first scene of Act II of *Troilus and Cressida* is not unlike Shakespeare's procedure in *1 Henry IV*, *Hamlet*, or *King Lear* in which II.i in each of these plays presents what can be called the world beneath the world of the play. Act II.i displays the nastiness that lies underneath the public Greek world in I.iii. This Greek subplot is filled with accusation, invective, slander: power without love or wisdom. Following II.i is the Trojan II.ii. On either side of II.i is a public scene, first the Greeks, then the Trojans. Act II.i, therefore, is bracketed by these public scenes and indicates the world beneath the public world of both sides of the conflict. We will see the ugliness beneath the public world of the Trojans verified when Margarelon, the bastard son of Priam, appears on the battlefield in V.vii. In both the Trojan and the Greek worlds, there is a "putrefied core" (V.viii.1).

If with Troilus in I.i and with Cressida I.ii we see love without wisdom and power and if the Greek council of I.iii presents wisdom without love or power, then II.i, the Achilles scene, presents power without love or wisdom. Act I.iii and II.i, two Greek scenes, fill out the concept presented in I.i and I.ii, two Trojan scenes. This Greek world corresponds to the Trojan world, which we see in I.i, Troilus's scene, and in I.ii, Cressida's scene. Ajax and Achilles disagree over

Thersites. Act II.ii, however, provides the Trojan viewpoint. Hector controls the end of this world, but we see that Ulysses has already subverted his end or good. By working in this way, Shakespeare manages to iterate the problem of the play through different and differing viewpoints, from five different viewpoints. The main point is that Hector wants the war to continue so that he can meet and defeat Achilles, but Ulysses, through his actions in the Greek council of I.iii, has already decided that Hector must fight Ajax, the man who has already defeated him. Hector acts the way he does in the Trojan council of II.ii because of his defeat at the hands of Ajax; the effect of Hector's behavior in II.ii will result, because of Ulysses's action, in his fighting Ajax again, something that Hector does not want. He wants to fight Achilles as a way of removing the stain of having been defeated by Ajax. Thus we see how foolish, sordid, and small-minded all the Greeks and the Trojans really are.

NOTES

1. Kenneth Muir, ed., *Troilus and Cressida* (Oxford: Oxford Univ. Press, 1984), 20. Muir elsewhere notes the following:

> One reason why *Troilus and Cressida* has been interpreted in so many different ways is that we are continually made to change our point of view. In nearly all the other plays we look at the action through the eyes of one or two closely related characters. We see *Hamlet* through Hamlet's eyes, never through those of Claudius; *King Lear* through Lear's eyes—or Cordelia's, or Kent's—but never through the eyes of Goneril; *The Tempest* through Prospero's eyes. It is true that another point is often given, and a character such as Horatio or Enobarbus may sometimes act as chorus. But in *Troilus and Cressida* the point of view is continually changing. . . . we distort the play if we make any one character to be Shakespeare's mouthpiece (*Aspects of Shakespeare's 'Problem Plays'* [Cambridge: Cambridge Univ. Press, 1982], 105).

Although Muir considers this strategy to be unique to *Troilus and Cressida*, it is not so anomalous as it at first appears. Consider Emrys Jones on *1 Henry IV*:

> we are never allowed to become identified with the point of view of any one of its characters. . . . The play's vision of reality is never less than complex: all viewpoints are partial. . . . We are presented with a number of conflicting voices, and although it is possible to pick out some

exceptionable sentiments . . . few positions are not exposed to the
questioning gaze of other positions nearby (*The Origins of Shakespeare*
[Oxford: The Clarendon Press, 1977], 13-14).

2. For a comparison of *Troilus and Cressida* to *King Lear* and to *Romeo and Juliet*, see
John Russell Brown, *Shakespeare and his Comedies* (London: Methuen, 1962).

3. Herbert Howarth correctly observes that Ulysses's statement on degree should not be
seen as expressing the "thinking of the time . . . without pause" (*The Tiger's Heart: Eight
Essays on Shakespeare* [New York: Oxford Univ. Press, 1970], 176).

4. See Milton Boone Kennedy, *The Oration in Shakespeare* (Chapel Hill: The Univ. of
North Carolina Press, 1942). Kennedy studies the rhetorical and oratory devices in
Shakespeare. Ulysses's speech in I.iii is seen as Shakespeare's greatest example of oration.
This misses the interpretive point, however.

5. "The debate in Troy enables the poet to show that the blame must be shared by all
the Trojan leaders; and the Greek heroes are all presented in as unflattering light as
possible" (Kenneth Muir, *Aspects of Shakespeare's 'Problem Play's: Articles Reprinted
from Shakespeare Survey* [Cambridge: Univ. Press, 1982], 99).

6. Camille Slights is excellent on the design of the play, noting that the parallel structure
of the council scenes (I.iii and II.ii) constitutes "one of the dominant parallel patterns in
the dramatic design" ("The Parallel Structure of *Troilus and Cressida*," *Shakespeare
Quarterly* 25 [1974]: 43).

7. Useful discussions of parallel structure in *Troilus and Cressida* are Harold S. Wilson,
On the Design of Shakespearean Tragedy (Toronto, 1957) and Joyce Carol Oates, "The
Ambiguity of Troilus and Cressida," *Shakespeare Quarterly* 17 (1966): 141-50.

8. See n. 1 above.

9. See Ralph Berry, *The Shakespearean Metaphor: Studies in Language and Form*
(Totowa, New Jersey: Roman and Littlefield, 1978). He calls the speeches in the two
council scenes into question.

10. Mirror is a term used by Hereward T. Price. There are scenes in Shakespeare's
plays, he writes, that "bring everything into focus," . . . Shakespeare's technique is to
construct a play by joining incident to incident. Each incident is a miniature play,"
("Mirror-Scenes in Shakespeare," in *Joseph Quincy Adams Memorial Studies*, ed. James
F. McManaway [Washington: Folger Shakespeare Library, 1948], 101-13). Although he
uses the term in a slightly different manner, Price's comment is decidedly related to the
notion of recapitulation.

11. The ideas expressed in the council scenes must be qualified by their context. "But
the question about the states and meaning of these 'ideas' are inseparable from questions
of who exactly is saying what exactly and in what particular context" (Jane Adamson,
"Drama in the Mind: Entertaining Ideas in *Troilus and Cressida*," *The Critical Review* 27
[1985], 6). Adamson's observation is useful. Clearly the context of the ideas expressed in
the council scenes belongs not only to the individual scene but also to its counterpart.

4

The Pandarus Scene

And hither am I come,
A Prologue arm'd, but not in confidence
Of author's pen or actor's voice, but suited
In like conditions as our argument,
To tell you, fair beholders, that our play
Leaps o'er the vaunt and firstlings of those broils,
Beginning in the middle, starting thence away
To what may be digested in a play.

(22-29)

Troilus and Cressida is thus introduced: an armed Prologue announces that the action will begin in the middle and that "our" play will be a digestion or a condensation of "those broils."[1] We are "fair beholders," as if we are fair or equitable or as if we are to behold what is fair or equitable. But we also seem to get the suggestion that the play is (or will become) like an Elizabethan fair. We can, I think, see why Shakespeare might want to give "us" as a base something with which we, as an Elizabethan audience, would be very familiar. "As an institution Bartholomew's fair existed for 700 years," notes Cornelius Walford.[2] Perhaps we are to view the Trojan War as if it were an Elizabethan fair: a place of animals and busy people; a place that emphasizes buying and selling; a place where someone like Cressida would be treated like a commodity. The animal and food imagery of the play, which we would associate with a fair, are by now commonplaces about the nature of this Shakespeare play.[3] At the end of IV.i, Paris comments:

> Fair Diomed, you do as chapmen do,
> Dispraise the thing that they desire to buy;
> But we in silence hold this virtue well,
> We'll not commend, that not intend to sell.
> Here lies our way.[4]
>
>   (IV.i.76-80)

Diomed is not, we guess, fair, either in complexion or in justice, yet he is behaving like a chapman, a person at a fair. Cressida, who will almost at once enter, is about to become a commodity: she will be used not valued. She has been exchanged for Antenor; her soliloquy in I.ii emphasizes her awareness of the nature of her present predicament: "'Achievement is command; ungain'd, beseech'" (I.ii.298).

The two titular characters, Troilus and Cressida, do not appear together on stage until III.ii, an orchard or garden scene, a "green world." Of the twenty-two scenes in the play, Troilus and Cressida are on stage together in only five of these scenes: III.ii; IV.ii; IV.iv; IV.v; V.ii. Act III.i, the scene that occurs right before the first Troilus-Cressida meeting, is strange and choric. As I have indicated, although the Prologue cites Paris and Helen as being most important, III.i is the only scene in which Helen, the cause of the war, appears: "The ravish'd Helen, Menelaus' queen,/With wanton Paris sleeps—and that's the quarrel" (9-10). That the cause of the war—Paris and Helen—appears immediately before the first appearance together on stage of Troilus and Cressida serves to relate Paris and Helen to Troilus and Cressida.[5] Immediately after the Prologue we get I.i, Troilus's scene, and then I.ii, Cressida's scene: the private plot. Again, immediately after III.i, we get the first scene in which Troilus and Cressida appear together on stage. Thus III.i is a kind of prologue for the dramatized Troilus-Cressida action.[6] Pandarus has come to Paris for Paris's help: "And my lord, [Troilus] desires you that if the King call for him at supper, you will make his excuse" (III.i.74-76). Troilus supported Paris in II.ii, the Trojan council scene; now Troilus is using Pandarus to get Paris to help him in his love cause.

Act III.i has three parts: Pandarus and a new character, a nameless servant, speak; Paris and Helen converse with Pandarus; Paris and Helen converse on stage after Pandarus has left. Indeed one of the features of this scene is the presentation of new characters, the nameless servant and Helen. Pandarus arrives at Priam's palace and is greeted by a man who is, presumably, Paris's servant in what is a kind of prologue to the entrance of Paris *and* Helen. The servant, in a manner very reminiscent of Feste in III.i as well as in IV.i of *Twelfth Night*, converses in a language different from that used up to now in the play: his idiom is different, strange; he pretends to misunderstand Pandarus. He deals in puns or clenches: "Sir, I do depend upon the Lord" (III.i.4); "The Lord be praised" (III.i.8); "You are in a state of grace" (III.i.14). The servant's disdain for Pandarus and indeed for Paris, his master, and Helen is evident. His last words in the episode and in the play are "Sodden business: there's a stewed phrase indeed!" (III.i.40-41) Upon these words Paris and Helen enter. It seems useful to distinguish the servant from Shakespeare. The servant disdains Pandarus, Paris, and Helen; by extension, he disdains Troilus and Cressida. Shakespeare may be said to employ the words of the servant to alert the audience to Christian considerations: *Lord, praise, grace.*[7] We, the audience, know of Christ, praise, and grace; the characters of *Troilus and Cressida* do not.[8] The implicit place for the servant's words would be a Christian church.[9] In effect then the referential strategy is not unlike the use of an Elizabethan fair.[10]

Thus the episode in III.i between Pandarus and the servant is both prologue and choric in that we see, though Pandarus does not, the Christian significance of the servant's speech. The words he uses emphasize the danger of uninstructed love, of cupid-love. The words introduce counters to vice and sin. When, later in the scene, Pandarus sings of love to Paris and Helen, we know that his love has been severely qualified by the servant's attitude and words; the Paris-Helen episode is a "sodden business" because of the context established by the conversation between Pandarus and the servant at the beginning of the scene: we are reminded of what we, as an Elizabethan audience, know about *grace, friendship, service, faith.*

Paris's first word in III.i is "fair," a word iterated eleven times in the first seven lines after his entrance. This "new" prologue reminds us again to be "fair beholders" (26) still. Since the trope of the Elizabethan fair is again invoked, we apparently are to view the second part of III.i as a fair. Thus III.i may be said to revise the prologue; or, to put it another way, III.i is an epilogue to the first part of the play, those Acts that, with the introduction of the significant characters and through the establishment of the important themes, provide us with all of the necessary information for an understanding of the rest of the play; with the Prologue, III.i brackets the action up to now. In any event, III.i is choric in that it emphasizes the Christian and human implications of the Troilus-Cressida action. We behold the fair rather than participate in it: we are to behold the sodden business with some detachment. We get a perversion of a church, for, as in *Much Ado About Nothing*, the church may be seen as a brothel, which is the way we are asked to see the setting of III.i. R.A. Foakes puts it thus:

> Helen teases [Pandarus], caresses him, distracts him from his business by continual interruptions, enforcing perhaps the quibble on "quean" in his words as he tries to disengage himself, "Sweet queen, sweet queen, there's a sweet queen i'faith. . . . What says my sweet queen, my very sweet queen?", and so on. She presumably returns to the embraces of Paris as they make him sing his song, "Love, love, nothing but love . . . "; but the love in this scene is nothing more than "hot blood, hot thoughts, and hot deeds", in the words of Pandarus, echoing Paris (III.i.125). The scene is gay and amusing, but the court of Troy is transmuted through this dialogue into a kind of high-class brothel, and love becomes another word for lechery.[11]

In the preceding Trojan scene (the public II.ii), Helenus, the priest, represents Trojan love or faith, as I have indicated. Although he is not a Christian priest, liturgically we can see him in a Christian light. As we look back from III.i to II.ii, having seen the advent of such prepossessive words as *faith* and *grace* in III.i, we can now see Helenus as being, in time, Christian. He is disregarded by Troilus there, just as Pandarus disregards the servant here in III.i. The servant in III.i, who invokes the Lord, honor, friendship, grace, is a choric figure like Helenus, the Trojan priest in II.ii. In II.ii Helenus is dismissed by Troilus; in III.i the servant, who may remain on stage as a silent character, is ignored by Paris and Helen. Once Paris and Helen come on stage, the servant is silent. Once Troilus in II.ii dismisses Helenus, Helenus remains on stage silent. Thus, as in II.ii, the one character in III.i who represents religious value is ignored but remains on stage. He is a silent choric figure, like Don John in I.i of *Much Ado About Nothing*. Again, III.i (like the Prologue) introduces the Troilus-Cressida action; it is a prologue to the "sodden Troilus-Cressida business." The full scene is choric; the second part or episode of the scene is choric in a different way from the first part in that it contains the only song in the play. Instead of words like *faith* and *grace*, we now hear *love*, cupid love, *"nothing but love"* (III.i.110), a word that is used nineteen times in III.i.

When Helenus in II.ii and the servant in III.i remain on stage, they become "fair beholders" of subsequent action in the scene. In this way they enable us to *measure* the other characters.[12] Act III.i presents the spectacle of Paris and Helen in the honey-sweet context of a brothel: it is "Sodden business."[13] The Ajax-Achilles action in II.i refers to the kind of animals found at a fair. This action is introduced at the end of I.iii: "Two curs shall tame each other: pride alone/Must tar the mastiffs on, as 'twere their bone" (I.iii.391-92). We are here (see the iteration of *fair*) to see Paris and Helen in the light of an Elizabethan fair. And considering the speech of the servant, we may see the "setting" as a church. Of course, we may also see the scene as a brothel.

In the elaborate context of fair-church-brothel, Shakespeare introduces the Troilus-Cressida action. The Troilus-Cressida action is conditioned by the context established in III.i. We are conditioned for the meeting between Troilus and Cressida. Paris and Helen help us to measure Troilus and Cressida. No one can seriously doubt that Helen ought to be given back to Menelaus. Still, the married Helen is a "mortal Venus," a living goddess; she is half-mortal; Cressida is only a girl. The Troilus-Cressida affair cannot be justified.

In III.i Pandarus sings the play's only song. Paris and Helen, who do not hear the servant's speech, hear the song. "*Love, love, nothing but love*" (III.i.110) has no power and wisdom: it isn't informed either by wisdom or by power. These lovers are outside the church, adulterers. Their love, without the wisdom of Christian love, is debased; again, no one can or does reasonably defend keeping Helen apart from her husband. That their love is indulgent and vulnerable is underlined by Paris's comment to Helen: "Sweet, above thought I love thee" (III.i.155). In III.i Pandarus is only Cupid; he sings Cupid's song. And his kind of love is, as I have said, a prologue to the beginning of the Troilus-Cressida action in III.ii. Perhaps it should be acknowledged that cupid-love may develop into a higher love. Troilus and Cressida are still innocent; they love each other. True love, sanctioned by marriage, would save them. But from another point of view, Paris and Helen are not as vulnerable as are Troilus and Cressida, for the war will continue. The Paris and Helen love affair is open, acknowledged, whereas, as we discover, both Troilus and Cressida want to keep their love affair secret.

Paris and Helen have Pandarus sing to them. Pandarus's song is followed by Paris's request of Helen to unarm Hector. He wants Hector to be unarmed so that his "sodden business" may continue. Like Troilus in I.i, Paris would rather wallow in love than be on the battlefield. Like Troilus, Paris puts love above thought. Although they must be aware of the public danger to Troy, the war means nothing to them; their understanding of love is honey-sweet and soft: strangely, the word *sweet* is used eighteen times in III.i.

The language of III.i suggests that we first think of a Christian community, then of a fair, then of a brothel. We may say that the setting of III.i is then like a church, a fair, a brothel. The tropes accrue. We come to III.ii with the tropes firmly established. After the first and only Paris-Helen spectacle, we begin the Pandarus-Troilus-Cressida spectacle. With these tropes in mind, we may now witness the Troilus-Cressida action with a knowledge of Shakespeare's qualifications.

But out of the more generalized trope of the church-fair-brothel, a particularized trope can be discerned, the trope of the bee. The prologue invokes a fair. Act I.i verbalizes the Pandarus-Troilus trope of bread. Act I.ii presents the dramatic Cressida trope of a procession. By means of the emphasis on *sweet*, III.i invokes the trope of the bee; we may refer to it as Pandarus's trope to distinguish it from the Pandarus-Troilus trope or from the Cressida trope. The trope of the bee, which we may then identify with Pandarus in III.i (Troilus or Cressida is not present), will recur, as we might expect, in Pandarus's epilogue-like comment in V.x:

> Full merrily the humble-bee doth sing
> Till he hath lost his honey and his sting;
> And being once subdu'd in armed tail,
> Sweet honey and sweet notes together fail.
>
> (V.x.42-45)

As we have determined, the first five scenes are recapitulative scenes. Act III.i may be said to be Pandarus's scene, comparable, in recapitulative terms, to the first five scenes of the play. The Pandarus scene of III.i emphasizes the honey-sweet product of the beehive; V.x will add the sting as a corollary to the bee metaphor: it emphasizes the necessary unpleasantness or danger of a humble bee. The trope of the bee further suggests that Helen may be seen as the queen bee, honey-sweet, around whom all must gather and serve, the reason for which the hive exists. Troy is seen by the Prologue as having "strong immures" (8), as if Troy is a kind of beehive, where Helen, the queen bee, resides. Just as the hive exists for the bee community, the war "exists" for Helen.[14] She is the cause and reason for the war; as the queen-bee, the war and community exist for her.[15]

The products of a beehive are honey and wax, sweetness and light. Sweetness represents one aspect of love, as III.i demonstrates, and light represents another aspect of love, *knowledge* or *awareness*. Light is not mentioned in III.i: "above thought I love thee" (III.i.155). By the end of the play, the sting will be added to or will replace sweetness and light. Or, to put it another way, these good products, sweetness and light, are qualified by the sting. In any event, in III.i the emphasis is on sweet love; in III.ii the emphasis is on light. Love, that attribute of the Apple of Discord possessed by the Trojans, is only implicitly good; it becomes good only when it is corrected and instructed. Uncorrected, uninstructed love can be destructive. Love informed by the tenets of Christianity—friendship, grace, service, faith, as indicated by the servant at the beginning of III.i—is good. Sweetness is good, but it is debased in III.i. Light is good, but, as we will see, it is not serviceable in III.ii.

Again, we "approach" the liaison between Troilus and Cressida through the liaison between Paris and Helen. Troilus and Cressida will become a lesser Paris and Helen because their love is unsanctioned. Helen is married to Menelaus, and this prohibits any viable Paris-Helen relationship, as the debate in II.ii, the Trojan council scene, makes clear. The Trojans insist on the divorce of Helen and Menelaus. Paris is wanton: "Sweet, above thought I love thee" (III.i.155). Cupid-love can develop (may develop) into something good, but only with Troilus and Cressida. The Paris-Helen action, however, seems meant to assure us that it won't. Pandarus (love) ought to be informed by the servant (faith), but Pandarus does not hear what *only we*, the "fair beholders," can truly hear.

NOTES

1. *Troilus and Cressida*, along with *Romeo and Juliet*, *Henry V*, *Henry VIII*, and *The Two Noble Kinsmen*, begins with a Prologue. In *Troilus and Cressida*, as in these other plays, the Prologue serves to deliver information necessary for an informed understanding of the play. It not only prepares the audience for the action that will follow by establishing the setting but also, in the case of *Troilus and Cressida*, the Prologue makes clear the nature of the conflict that will follow, sets forth the tensions by establishing the opposing factions of the play, and indicates the compressed mode of the drama. For instance, we learn that the play is a digestion of the epic material; we discover that the war is between the Trojans and the Greeks; we determine the subject of the "quarrel." That Shakespeare uses a Prologue in *Troilus and Cressida* is an indication of the play's similarity to these other Shakespeare plays. It is a strategy that Shakespeare returns to throughout the canon. We can, for example, note that, although not strictly named as prologues, Rumor in *2 Henry IV*, the witches in *Macbeth*, and Gower in *Pericles* are all serving the function of prologues. Shakespeare's manner of using, in one form or another, a prologue to begin the play would indicate his belief in its usefulness. Thus in *Troilus and Cressida*, one of Shakespeare's most difficult plays, the Prologue serves as a strategy for rendering meaning. And this strategy is returned to, in one form or another, at various times in the play.

Although the Prologue names the source of the conflict between the Trojans and the

Greeks as Paris's involvement with Helen, the Greek queen, the title of the play, as I have noted, is *Troilus and Cressida*, the two Trojan lovers.

2. Cornelius Walford, *Fairs, Past and Present: A Chapter in the History of Commerce* (London: Elliot Stock, 1883), 167.

3. See Caroline F. E. Spurgeon, *Shakespeare's Imagery and What It Tells Us* (London: Cambridge Univ. Press, 1952).

4. The word *lies* here echoes the first line of the play: "In Troy there lies the scene." It provides the notion that the play that we are about to see is a complex web of lies, or, rather, depicts the Trojan War as a web of lies. Here the word suggests that Troilus and Cressida are also caught in the web and that they will suffer from its existence. They may be the *way*, a possible answer, but the answer that they provide will be debased. See n. 13 chap. 1 above.

5. Thomas B. Stroup recognizes the "well-defined" balance between the "love triangle of Troilus, and Cressida, and Diomedes" and its parallel, "the love triangle of Menelaus, Helen, and Paris" (*Microcosmos: The Shape of the Elizabethan Play* [Lexington: The Univ. of Kentucky Press, 1965], 64).

6. Rolf Soellner makes the point that the juxtaposition of III.i and III.ii makes III.i "a sardonic introduction to the love tryst of Troilus and Cressida, which follows immediately" (*Shakespeare's Patterns of Self-Knowledge* [Columbus: Ohio Univ. Press, 1972], 208). Clearly III.i is a prologue to III.ii.

7. David Kaula brings into focus the Christian implications of the text and notes that "Troy from the Virgilian standpoint was considered the forerunner of Rome" ("'Mad Idolatry' in Shakespeare's *Troilus and Cressida*," *Texas Studies in Literature and Language* 15 [1973]: 25-38). This also helps to clarify the point that Aeneas will be released by the fall of Troy to found Rome, which will bring the Christian notion of love.

8. Carolyn Asp, "Transcendence Denied: The Failure of Role assumption in *Troilus and Cressida*," *Studies in English Literature* 18 (1978): 257-74. Although Ms. Asp claims that the agent of transcendence in the play is art, I think that we should add that the Christian lessons, as implied by the servant and Pandarus in III.i, offer a possibility for a kind of transcendence, to use the term employed by Asp.

9. "Whenever Shakespeare repeatedly resorts to a certain terminology, . . . it is well to consider whether he might be presenting it as an implicit commentary on the attitudes he is dramatizing" (Kaula, "Mad Idolatry," 26). The words of the servant and Pandarus in III.i clearly refer to a church.

10. Once we see the Christian implications of III.i, we are admonished to see their implications in I.i and I.ii. In the play's first scene the primary trope is the baking of bread, which is discussed by Troilus and Pandarus. Having seen the Christian imagery in III.i, the scene with the song of love, we may recognize the Christian implications of the bread imagery in I.i. For the bread may be seen in Christian terms as the body of Christ, and the scene may even allude to the Last Supper, a recognition to which we come if we are aware of liturgical convention. We do not immediately see the allusion; it is made manifest after a thorough reading of the play and if we invest the scene (I.i) not only with the meaning the play will unfold but also with the meaning inherent in our perception. This

is like a liturgical reading of the Old Testament. We read a character as a type of Christ. This kind of investing pre-Christian fact with Christian meaning is a Renaissance commonplace. Troilus, like Cressida, is only human. His difficulty, precipitated by his importunity, thus presents him with an ethical and moral dilemma. Further, Cressida's soliloquy, so famous for its maxim delivered "out of love," is extended in its implications by our new understanding of the Christian implications and the new lesson of love. In a fractured world such as that in *Troilus and Cressida*, Love, Power, and Wisdom, the attributes of the goddesses, will not be brought together without the fall of Troy.

11. See R.A. Foakes, *Shakespeare: The Dark Comedies to the Last Plays* (Charlottesville: Univ. Press of Virginia, 1971), 53.

12. *Much Ado About Nothing* provides precedent for our being able to measure one character by another. In II.iii we hear of Beatrice's letter in which she says that she measures Benedick by her own spirit.

13. "Shakespeare's Helen is more than faded," writes Douglas Cole, "she is tarnished and tawdry. . . . What Shakespeare does to Helen is emblematic of what he does with the heroic strain of the Trojan War in general" ("Myth and Anti-Myth: The Case of *Troilus and Cressida*," *Shakespeare Quarterly* 31 [1980]: 76).

14. See Susanne K. Langer, *Mind: An Essay on Human Feeling*, 2 vols. (Baltimore: The Johns Hopkins Univ. Press, 1972). Ms. Langer comments on the inadequacy of the beehive as a metaphor for the human community.

15. The rape of Helen is like the rape of the flower by the bee. The fall of Troy will occur because the Trojans will bring the famous wooden horse into the city. As Paris brings Helen into the city so the Trojans will admit the horse. Troilus will engage in the symbolic action of going out and returning in the scenes that follow. The rape of Helen by Paris is like the rape of the city by the Greeks. Yeats' famous poem "Leda and the Swan" makes clear this historical distinction. The trope of the bee asks us to recognize the various implications of the abduction of Helen.

5

The Troilus and Cressida Scenes

Troilus and Cressida meet in III.ii—Cressida's first scene after I.ii, the scene in which she reveals her essential self in a famous soliloquy—and here they make clear their feelings to each other. This is the obligatory Troilus-Cressida scene, coming immediately after the Paris-Helen "prologue scene" of III.i. Although she has told us in I.ii that she has misled Pandarus about her feelings for Troilus and although she has stated that she will submit to Troilus, strangely, Cressida has become the aggressor.

Pandarus and, according to the stage direction, Troilus's Man open III.ii; Troilus enters; Pandarus brings Cressida to Troilus; Troilus and Cressida walk alone in the orchard; Pandarus re-enters, sends the lovers to consummate their vows, and delivers a final couplet: "And Cupid grant all tongue-tied maidens here/Bed, chamber, pander to provide this gear" (III.ii 209-10). Troilus has two soliloquies. Pandarus leaves the stage in order, so he says, to get fire, leaving Troilus and Cressida on a presumably darkened stage. After both Troilus and Cressida express their love, Pandarus re-enters with fire or light. The expression of love between Troilus and Cressida, therefore, takes place on stage *in the dark*. As we have seen, sweetness is emphasized in III.i; now the absence of light is emphasized in III.ii. Sweetness is one good product of the beehive; wax is the second good product. Like Paris and Helen, Troilus and Cressida express sweetness, but light is absent: "Sweet, above thought I love thee" (III.i.155). Love without knowledge or understanding is vulnerable, debased, dangerous.

Cressida uses the same words to invite Troilus into the orchard that she uses to invite him into the house: "Will you walk in, my lord" (III.ii.60,98). Cressida's words echo Psalm 23 and emphasize light and faith. The point is that Troilus and Cressida are *in the dark* on stage during their interchange, the same strategy Shakespeare uses, for instance, in IV.ii of *Twelfth Night* where Olivia's house is as dark as ignorance, hell, Egypt. Troilus and Cressida are ignorant, benighted. Cressida's question brackets the expression of love in the orchard and, therefore, may be seen as a reference to faith, like the servant's words in III.i. We are meant to see Cressida's remarks in III.ii (granted the choric nature of III.i) in a religious context that qualifies the onstage action. Without seeing III.i as a prologue, we might not see the biblical reference: the light in III.ii may perhaps be extended to refer to Christ as the light of the world. This conversation is symbolically qualified by a consideration of the Lord, just as the servant's words in III.i help us to understand and to qualify the action of Pandarus, Paris, and Helen. Shakespeare is asking us to read the Troilus-Cressida action in the orchard in the light of our knowledge of the Old Testament Lord and then in its Christian sense. Troilus and Cressida, however, do not and *cannot* "walk in [the shadow of the] Lord." They are not biblical. Rather than walking in the shadow of the Lord, Troilus and Cressida walk in the shadow of Cupid-love. Again, the first Troilus-Cressida scene, III.ii, is introduced by III.i, and III.i, as we have seen, is begun by Pandarus and the nameless servant. Pandarus in III.i provides one kind of answer with his song, the answer of nothing but love. For his answer is Cupid-love: it has no power or wisdom, and in III.ii he is off stage while Troilus and Cressida exchange their vows of Cupid-love. Pandarus's love must be qualified, instructed, and corrected by Old Testament love, by an understanding of sacrifice, and then by the discipline of Christian love. We must see the sacrificial nature of the Troilus-Cressida action in order to understand the human implications of the mythic story. We are meant to understand the full nature of the failure of Troilus and Cressida. Troilus lets Cressida go. In fact, when Cressida is summoned to the exchange in IV.ii, the next Troilus-Cressida scene, she is referred to by Aeneas as a "sacrifice" (IV.ii.66), a term that she herself uses in her soliloquy in I.ii. But Troilus doesn't know Christ. He is only love without power and wisdom; he is part of a known story, the historical story of Troilus and Cressida. Troilus's "drama" is limited and conditioned, for he is part of a dramatized spectacle. Troilus, Cressida, and Pandarus are unaware that they are filling predetermined roles, as Pandarus reminds us at the end of III.ii:

> If ever you prove false one to another, since I have
> taken such pains to bring you together, let all
> pitiful goers-between be called to the world's end
> after my name: call them all Pandars: let all
> constant men be Troiluses, all false women
> Cressids, and all brokers-between Pandars. Say
> 'Amen'.
>
> (III.ii.197-203)

We may see Troilus and Cressida, along with Hero and Leander, as one of the patterns of love, as *As You Like It* and *Much Ado About Nothing* make clear.[1] Then, as a pattern of love, Troilus and Cressida may be seen as a kind of trope. The trope of the Apple of Discord separates love from wisdom and power; the trope of the bee separates love into sweetness and light. The modern tropes of the church, the fair, the brothel qualify the trope of the Troilus and Cressida story which, as a story, is a trope for the Trojan War and leads us back to and away from the Apple of Discord.

* * *

Aeneas comes with a knock in IV.ii to inform Troilus of the exchange of Cressida for Antenor. In effect his knocking "kills" Pandarus as he replaces Pandarus in the private plot, a replacement that is reflected in the design of I.i, Troilus's first scene. After Troilus's soliloquy in I.i, Aeneas enters with an alarm. Pandarus has an effect in Act III (he brings Troilus and Cressida together); Aeneas has an effect in Act IV (he brings about the exchange of Antenor for Cressida). But still nothing positive happens. Although we can see the possibility of a solution (Aeneas's higher love replaces Pandarus's lower love), that solution becomes impossible in part because Troilus doesn't rise to the occasion, which is unlike a Shakespeare comedy in which the solution is realized and concord is achieved. Aeneas is performing a public function: unlike Pandarus, he is detached, a better servant. If the tropes of III.i were reversed (brothel, fair, church), then a good end could result.

Once Aeneas in IV.ii informs Troilus and Cressida of the impending exchange, Troilus leaves to go to Paris, his brother, in order to discover the details. While Troilus is gone, Cressida protests:

> I will not, uncle. I have forgot my father;

> I know no touch of consanguinity,
> No kin, no love, no blood, no soul so near me
> As the sweet Troilus! O you gods divine,
> Make Cressid's name the very crown of falsehood
> If ever she leave Troilus! Time, force, and death,
> Do to this body what extremes you can;
> But the strong base and building of my love
> Is as the very centre of the earth,
> Drawing all things to it. I'll go in and weep—
>   (IV.ii.99-108)

After Pandarus speaks and exits, she continues:

> —Tear my bright hair, and scratch my praised cheeks,
> Crack my clear voice with sobs, and break my heart
> With sounding 'Troilus'. I will not go from Troy.
>   (IV.ii.110-12)

Troilus does not hear Cressida's protest at the end of IV.ii because he is off stage seeing Paris. If he were to hear, he might act differently. Pandarus knows, and the audience knows; Troilus is denied this light, denied this knowledge. "How my achievements mock me" (IV.ii.71) reveals his conceit and his cowardice. It is a response that echoes Cressida's "philosophy" as expressed in her soliloquy in I.ii: "'Achievement is command; ungain'd, beseech'" (I.ii.298). Both of these statements imply the close relationship of love to war: love is expressed in terms of war and war in terms of love. For, again, the private plot echoes and mirrors the public plot.

* * *

Troilus is not present at the beginning of IV.iv. Cressida again demonstrates her grief to Pandarus in answer to his advice that she be moderate:

> The grief is fine, full, perfect, that I taste,
> And violenteth in a sense as strong
> As that which causeth it: how can I moderate it?
> If I could temporize with my affection,
> Or brew it to a weak and colder palate,

> The like allayment could I give my grief.
> My love admits no qualifying dross,
> No more my grief, in such a precious loss.
> (IV.iv.3-10)

Again, as with Cressida's speeches of protest in IV.ii, Troilus is not aware of how Cressida feels; he does not hear and see either her protest or her grief. This lack of knowledge, this lack of light, affects Troilus's behavior and response.

In IV.iv Pandarus refers to Troilus and Cressida as "a pair of spectacles" (IV.iv.13), indicating the spectacle, the pageant of Troilus and Cressida as they proceed toward Troilus's "necessary" rejection of Cressida in Act V. As Pandarus pronounces the young lovers as spectacles, he embraces them both. This action emphasizes, as does the end of III.ii, that their fate is sealed. The fate of all three is inevitably, historically linked: Pandarus, Cressida, Troilus—all three will fail and fall in turn. As I have indicated, we may see the play as a spectacle, just as we may see the *Aeneid* as a kind of spectacle.

But by referring to them as a *pair* of spectacles, Pandarus indicates that Troilus and Cressida must be used as a means of seeing, as a means of focusing the action. I should therefore like to suggest that the spectacle is a kind of trope for understanding the play. Troilus and Cressida are like spectacles, glasses. We are to use the Troilus-Cressida story as the agent of mediation. Troilus, Cressida, and Pandarus are the central reference figures. The emphasis in III.ii and IV.i is upon seeing and light. Act III.ii, IV.i, and IV.iv, for instance, emphasize light (Troilus and Cressida are in the dark in the orchard), and sight (Aeneas opens IV.i with "See, ho!"). We can say that glasses can enable sight. But because Troilus and Cressida have no light in III.ii, they are willing to obey Pandarus, willing to submit to Cupid-love. The trope of fire-light is refined into glasses, just as the trope of wisdom-power-love is refined into sweetness and light. Or, to put it another way, glasses are added to the trope of fire-light, just as the sting is added to sweetness and light. Now if Troilus and Cressida were able to see that their fates are linked (they are a pair of spectacles; they do love each other), then, possibly, they would be able to see both the difficulties and the possibilities of their relationship. This is not an unusual Shakespeare procedure; in *Much Ado About Nothing*, for example, Shakespeare again emphasizes spectacles with the "eye of love" and the "eye of favor"; once true love is achieved, seeing is made possible, as Beatrice's comment that she "can see a church by daylight" (II.i.82-83) indicates. But in *Troilus and Cressida*, true love may not be achieved, as V.iii, the scene in which Troilus tears up the letter from Cressida, determines.

* * *

In IV.v we are led to expect the entrance of Hector to the Greek camp, but Cressida enters instead: Hector is announced; Cressida appears. Just as, we may say, Aeneas follows Pandarus in IV.ii, so Hector follows Cressida in IV.v. As Aeneas replaces Pandarus, so Cressida replaces Hector. To put it another way, just as we equate Aeneas and Pandarus, so we are to equate Cressida and Hector. All four are from Troy. Aeneas is a higher form of love than Pandarus. Cressida's love may become a higher form of love than Hector's. However, Cressida represents debased love; Hector represents debased honor. Just as in the private, love plot love is distinguished as sweetness and light, so in the public, war plot Cressida, a replacement for Antenor, is distinguished as debased love as opposed to debased honor. Cressida is a victim of the private plot, the love plot; Hector is a victim of the public plot, the war plot. Both of them, we may say, mean well, but both eventually find themselves victims.

The action of kissing each leader, except for Menelaus, in turn is a variation of the Cressida trope of the procession, which we are given in I.ii as Cressida watches the returning Trojan soldiers; it is thus a revision of I.ii. There Cressida watches the Trojan warriors; here she kisses the Greek warriors. When Patroclus intervenes in the kiss intended for Menelaus with "For thus popp'd Paris in his hardiment,/And parted thus you and your argument" (IV.v.28-29), the relationship between the Paris-Helen-Menelaus action and the Troilus-Cressida-Diomedes action is emphasized. The confrontations in IV.v are clear in their implications. We are meant to perceive that now Love, in the form of Cressida, has gone over to the Greek camp, but to no good end. For it is uninformed and uncorrected; it is only an application of the error of Helen's abduction, now on a less than epic level. Unlike Helen's husband, Menelaus, Troilus—Cressida's frail "husband"—hands her over to the Greeks. Cressida has been discarded and sacrificed. The failure of Troilus and Cressida to "hold off" has resulted in their desperate situation. Yet their desperation is a reflection of the larger public desperation involved in the public conflict; the Troilus-Cressida action is a gloss on the public action, spectacles to and for that action. Thus the public and the private plots, re-enforced by the Cressida-Hector equation, come together in a dramatic way in IV.v.

Not only have Cressida and Hector gone over to the Greeks in IV.v but also has Troilus. Thus love has gone over to the Greeks, has "joined" wisdom and power. But, as we have seen, love and honor have been discredited. Troilus has not acted honorably. True wisdom and real power have to be joined with true love. The movement of these Trojans to the Greek camp is a kind of a mockery of the possibilities suggested by the joining of love with power and wisdom. We may say that in IV.ii Troilus, Cressida, and Pandarus represent Shakespeare's pervasive trope: the head, the heart, the hand. Aeneas replaces Pandarus as the hand, for Pandarus operates as the instrument of change in the private plot, and when Aeneas comes to inform Troilus of Cressida's impending exchange, he "replaces" Pandarus in this role. And here in IV.v, we may say that *Hector* has also become the hand, an instrument for public change. Thus the mockery of the Apple of Discord trope, as suggested by the movement of the Trojans to the Greek camp, is extended to a mockery of the trope of the body.

Troilus ends IV.v by saying to Ulysses,

> O sir, to such as boasting show their scars
> A mock is due. Will you walk on, my lord?
> She was belov'd, she lov'd; she is, and doth;
> But still sweet love is food for fortune's tooth.
> (IV.v.289-92)

The references to *sweet* and "will you walk on, my lord" suggest a relationship between IV.v and III.i, the Pandarus-Paris-Helen scene, and III.ii, the Pandarus-Troilus-Cressida scene. Act III.i and III.ii establish the trope of the bee with its emphasis on sweetness (love) and light (knowledge). Here in IV.v Troilus is in the process of giving up sweetness (his love for Cressida), and he has no light (no real understanding). The light, as qualified by the servant in III.i, may be seen as Christ, the light of the world. In III.ii Cressida asks Troilus to "walk in, my lord?" (III.ii.60,98) In IV.v Troilus asks Ulysses to "walk on, my lord?" (IV.v.290) Obviously, "Walk on, my lord" is a revision of "walk in, my lord." In III.ii we may say that the lord is Christ or an understanding of Christ, an understanding of the lesson of the higher love of Christ, as indicated by the servant's words. The effect of Troilus's question in IV.v is to indicate that to walk in the shadow of the lord, to walk in the light of Christ, has, in effect, become a walk *on* the Lord.

* * *

In V.ii and *in the light* are Diomedes and Cressida. Watching Diomedes and Cressida from the shadows are Troilus and Ulysses. Thersites watches all four, Diomedes and Cressida, and Troilus and Ulysses. The audience in the theater or the reader in the study watches Thersites watching Troilus and Ulysses, who watch Diomedes and Cressida. The staging establishes levels of awareness. Diomedes and Cressida are unaware of Troilus and Ulysses. Troilus and Ulysses are unaware of Thersites. The stage here is like a painting that must be read visually.

As a symbolic prop light is important in III.ii, IV.i, and V.ii. Its symbolic context is still awareness, knowledge, understanding. In this context, Troilus and Cressida represent separated love in V.ii. We move from spectacle in IV.v to stage performance in V.ii. The dramatic strategy is that of eavesdropping. Cressida is equated with Diomedes; Troilus is equated with Ulysses. Here the stage is used in order to emphasize levels of awareness: who knows what. As we might expect, the distance from the light, which shines from *Menelaus's* tent, signifies understanding and represents the levels of knowledge. Thersites, a beast, understands least: he is most in the dark, yet, ironically, he sees the others. He has no knowledge or faith. He has no wisdom, no power. He is a Greek: he has not seen anything of value. Now that the action of the play has moved to the Greek camp, Thersites has replaced Pandarus: Pandarus is debased love; Thersites is debased wisdom and power. Outside it all are the members of the audience; they know most, having seen all aspects of the play.

Because he is not present in IV.ii and IV.iv when Cressida is protesting and grieving, Troilus misunderstands Cressida's actions in V.ii. He is blind to the full context of her behavior. Now Troilus is equated with blind, faithless Ulysses. The proud Ulysses, the agent of Grecian guile, is Troilus's guide. Like Ulysses, Troilus no longer cares what others think: he is preoccupied with himself. And Ulysses's judgment of Cressida in IV.v as one of the "daughters of the game" (IV.v.63) is confirmed by his attitude in V.ii. By means of the equation of Troilus and Ulysses, the private plot and the public plot have come together: Cressida is Hector; Troilus is Ulysses. In IV.v Hector is equated with Cressida; in V.ii Ulysses is equated with Troilus. Act V.ii is a version of the play in visual terms, only now the light does not bracket the action, as in III.ii. Light is with Cressida and Diomedes; Troilus and Ulysses are some distance from the light.

Light may be understood, therefore, in several ways. In IV.v and III.ii light may be seen as the light of the Lord. Yet in V.ii light will become a palpable prop, one that informs our understanding of the implications of the setting. Still, light may be said to bracket, in one form or another, V.i, a scene in which Thersites practices invective in the presence of Achilles, which is comparable to Thersites's behavior in II.i. On one side of V.i we have the light of Christ; on the other side of V.i we have the important light as symbolic prop. To put it another way, V.i, another scene in which Thersites practices invective, is encompassed by light. Thersites knows least and acts most like an animal. Thus in the center of III.ii Troilus and Cressida are physically in the dark, without knowledge or understanding—love without wisdom and power—whereas in V.i Thersites is the product of darkness, the fool of war, wisdom and power without love. He knows least because he feels nothing. He has "replaced" Troilus and Cressida on stage as Shakespeare's means of rendering the dark implications of the separation of love from wisdom and power. His invective is darkest, most brutal. We now have, presented as a spectacle, a final dramatic statement of the Troilus and Cressida situation.

When watching Cressida and Diomedes in V.ii, Troilus remarks: "This is, and is not, Cressid" (V.ii.145). Although capable of seeing two Cressidas, Troilus is not aware of a third Cressida, the grieving girl. Troilus has not heard Cressida's "philosophy" as expressed in I.ii. He has heard her importunity only in III.ii; he has heard the *fair* Cressida and the *brothel* Cressida, but not the *church* Cressida. Moreover, I should like to suggest that, because of the offstage action in III.iii, that of the consummation of the vows exchanged between Troilus and Cressida, her position is more desperate than even she knows. We may call this the human trope. She is now a prisoner of the Greeks, and as a prisoner she has little privilege; she must do what she can to preserve herself. Troilus, who may have love, has no wisdom, wisdom that he has no way of having, just as he does not know Christian wisdom, which is Christian power through love. What Troilus sees in V.ii is a girl in jeopardy, and he is not sufficiently aware of her desperate position. He should see some way of reconciling the three Cressidas. But he cannot. The play insists that wisdom, power, and love be joined, that sweetness and light be joined. The answer would be for Troilus to see the real Cressida. But he does not fully understand or appreciate her position. He knows only the importunate girl of III.ii, the *fair* and *brothel* Cressida. Thus IV.ii and IV.iv provide the information necessary for us to understand what Troilus cannot know. He has limited information; he does not fully know Cressida. In other words, there are kinds of levels of awareness: Troilus has partial knowledge; we have the knowledge of the Bible (the Old Testament and the New Testament), the *Aeneid*, the Troilus-Cressida story.

Troilus, as a young man, should not have been so importunate (though Cressida wants him too) in III.ii; he could have "married" her in Act IV; he discards her in Act V. But because in various ways Troilus lacks the light of knowledge, he is not effective. We know that he cannot change that which is unchangeable, documented, known. He should be a thematic stage beyond both Pandarus and Aeneas. Pandarus would serve himself by uniting Cressida, his niece, and Troilus, a member of the royal family; Aeneas, as I.i, I.iii, and IV.v indicate, would serve Hector; Troilus should serve Cressida, but, again, he is trapped in several distinguishable ways.

It seems significant that Act III begins with music, that Act IV begins with light, that Act V begins with a sword. These "props," which begin the final three Acts of the play, may aid our understanding. They indicate that the movement is from *music*, which begins the third Act, to *light*, which begins the fourth Act, to a *sword*, which begins the fifth Act. We may see them as a translation of the head-heart-hand trope in symbolic terms. But they are out of order. We may say that the proper order of the props, if Troilus and Cressida were successful, ought to be the *sword*, the *light*, the *music*, a movement toward concord, a movement suggested by the reversal of the brothel-fair-church trope. It is as if the play goes backwards. In these terms the last three Acts of the play move from the New Testament in III.i, to the Old Testament in IV.i, to the Greeks in Act V. This is the procedure Shakespeare uses in *Hamlet*, that of a backward movement: "if like a crab you could go backward" (II.ii.203-04).

* * *

Five different times Troilus and Cressida appear on stage in the same scene; these five scenes chart the course of their relationship. As soon as Troilus and Cressida are hustled off to bed in III.ii, Calchas arranges to get his daughter back. As soon as Troilus and Cressida are committed to each other, morning tests them. Troilus and Cressida have no time together. If Cressida were not to surrender to Troilus in III.ii, her value would not diminish. She *must go* to the Greeks, however, unless Troilus, her frail "husband," prevents it. If they were married, he could prevent it. Troilus and Cressida have three encounters, one each in III.ii, IV.ii, IV.iv. In IV.v and V.ii, they are on stage but no encounter takes place. In IV.v Troilus and Cressida appear on stage at different times; in V.ii they are both on stage at the same time but Cressida is unaware of Troilus's presence.

As III.i is a prologue to III.ii, so IV.i is a prologue IV.ii. In III.i Pandarus, as the singer of the song, serves a choric function. In IV.i Aeneas, by his actions, serves a choric function. Pandarus serves Troilus and Cressida; Aeneas serves Hector. Thus Aeneas can submit himself to a higher service, for, unlike Pandarus, Aeneas has nothing to gain by his service. Pandarus, as surrogate father, betrays Cressida. Aeneas does not commit this betrayal, although we know that he will betray Dido. Still, it is Aeneas who, as messenger, brings the news of Cressida's separation from Troilus; by this action he tests them. The fourth Act opens with Aeneas's use of the phrase "heavenly business" (IV.i.5), which counters the "Sodden business" (III.i.40) of III.i. Aeneas "knocks Pandarus in the head" in IV.ii: Pandarus represents Cupid-love; Aeneas is the real son of Venus, love. He is an instrument of the public plot: in exchanging Cressida for Antenor, he carries out orders. This provides an opportunity for Troilus, which Troilus fails to seize, for in failing to make public his affair with Cressida, Troilus fails to stop the exchange. Pandarus gives way to Aeneas, who will have the future documented in and by the *Aeneid*. Once Troy falls, his story may and can begin. It will point to the founding of Rome, which in time will become the center of Christianity. Thus Aeneas, who provides the test for Troilus with the news of Cressida's exchange, a test that Troilus fails to seize, begins a new movement in IV.i; on the level of story, he provides a way out of the impasse at which we arrive in Act III.[2] During the course of III.ii, IV.ii, and IV.iv, Troilus and Cressida are apart for brief moments, as Troilus goes out and returns with confirmation of the impending exchange. Ironically, the news with which Troilus returns will in time turn him from sweetness to bitter revenge, a sting that he deeply feels. In part, he fails because of his limited love. But he also doesn't have time, for, as we have seen, plans are made for the exchange of Cressida as soon as Troilus and Cressida are committed. Morning comes and catches him unprepared. Troilus is never able to get beyond himself, as V.ii, Troilus's eavesdropping scene, and V.iii, the scene in which he tears up Cressida's letter, indicate. The Troilus-Cressida relationship happens so quickly that the two do not have time to know each other.

Troilus has no way of knowing the full Troilus-Cressida story, and he does not see Aeneas as the symbolic representative of a higher level of love or as the hero of the *Aeneid*, just as Pandarus does not know the New Testament in III.ii; thus for Troilus to grow through this kind of recognition is impossible. Our knowledge of the Bible, the *Aeneid*, the Troilus-Cressida story, however, is necessary for an understanding of the Troilus-Cressida action in the play. The "replacement" of one character by another is a dominant feature of the action. For instance, Aeneas, as we have seen, replaces Pandarus in IV.ii. Diomedes replaces Troilus at the side of Cressida. Troilus replaces Hector as the central Trojan warrior. Thersites replaces Troilus and Cressida as the means of demonstrating the implications of love without wisdom and power.

In V.ii Troilus, who, as we have seen, is not present when Cressida displays her grief in IV.iv, does not understand what he is witnessing. He, like all of the Trojans and the Greeks, is not fully aware of the sacrificial implications of the loss of Cressida. The symbolic implications of the setting in V.ii are apparent. Cressida, the Trojan sacrifice, is nearest to the light. Cressida, contrary to what critics have traditionally argued, is not merely one of the "daughters of the game"

(IV.v.63), as Ulysses says; rather, she is one of the symbolic representatives of the loss and destruction brought about by the war; moreover, she is fulfilling her particular role in the Troilus and Cressida pattern of love. Troilus is another sacrifice and is fulfilling his story too. And as the Prologue indicates, we may see this loss in terms of an Elizabethan fair in which the emphasis is placed upon commodity, a term that Cressida fully understands, for she has now been converted into just a commodity, a term that defines the reduction of human value by the public conflict.

NOTES

1. In both plays, *Much Ado About Nothing* and *As You Like It*, Shakespeare links Troilus and Cressida and Hero and Leander; he has Rosalind in *As You Like It* refer to the couples as "patterns of love" (IV.i.100).

2. Aeneas performs a similar function in I.i. In the first scene Pandarus leaves Troilus on stage. After Troilus's soliloquy, Aeneas enters and urges Troilus to accompany him to battle. The impasse at which Troilus arrives in the first scene, that of being unable to fight, that of being "weaker than a woman's tear" (I.i.9), is resolved with the help of Aeneas.

6

The Achilles Scene

The first Troilus and Cressida scene, III.ii, is the end of the first part of the Troilus and Cressida action: they leave the stage in order to go to bed together; their relationship will now be consummated. What begins in I.i and I.ii reaches an end in III.ii. But we do not get in III.iii a bedroom scene, which we might expect. In such a complex, condensed play as *Troilus and Cressida* we may, not unexpectedly, get a new, different focus. One kind of major plot action is presented in III.ii; a different kind of plot action is presented in III.iii. But this procedure, which may seem strange, is in fact typical. The last scene of Act III of a Shakespeare play often deals, not with major plot action, but with what we may call choric action. To make the crucial point exactly, the next-to-the-last scene of Act III is often climactic and climacteric to plot action; in those instances the last scene of Act III is undeniably and primarily choric.

In *Richard II*, for example, as soon as Richard submits to Bolingbroke in III.iii (he capitulates and agrees to go to London), the famous choric scene of the garden is presented. Act III.iv establishes the centrality of the garden trope to our understanding of the action. It focuses on the Queen, not on Richard. In *Hamlet*, as soon as Hamlet is sure that the King is guilty, he comes upon the King at prayer but does not kill him (III.iii); the last scene of Act III (III.iv)—the re-appearance of the ghost and the killing of Polonius—is thus choric. Richard confronts Bolingbroke in III.iii of *Richard II*; Hamlet "confronts" Claudius in

III.iii of *Hamlet*. Because Hamlet does not kill Claudius, the action changes and continues. In *King Lear*, Lear reaches an end in III.vi: he falls asleep and is carried off stage to safety. The horrible blinding of Gloucester in III.vii deals, as in *Richard II* and *Hamlet*, with a close "relative" of the hero and is crucially choric.[1]

This procedure of presenting new action at the end of Act III allows Shakespeare to step back, as it were, and to ask us to ventilate or to explore a situation that has just reached a point of climax. For instance, III.iv of *Richard II* presents the garden and the gardener-king, notions that are introduced in II.i by Gaunt's famous speech: England is "This other Eden, demi-paradise" (II.i.42); Richard is not a true king. The king must care for this paradise like a gardener, not like a landlord. Act III.iv of *Hamlet* presents again the metaphoric and symbolic ghost who prompts the initial action. The return of the ghost is an essential choric assertion: Hamlet has not obeyed the Ghost's charge to kill the king. The outside force is re-introduced: its appeal, like that of the gardener-king, is re-stated. After meeting Claudius Hamlet meets the queen, Polonius (Claudius's surrogate), the other Hamlet. Act III.vii of *King Lear* clarifies the father-king trope, which is the essence of Lear's initial problem. It re-establishes the tension between his role as king and his role as father.[2]

Thus, in *Troilus and Cressida*, we are encouraged to view III.iii as primarily choric. The focus is not on Troilus and Cressida: the concern is on contextual considerations. Although III.iii portrays the plot action of Achilles and the Greek leaders, this scene serves also to ventilate the Troilus and Cressida position, which, as we have noted, is established in I.i and I.ii. It ventilates, for instance, the outside-inside trope of the first Troilus scene,

> Call here my varlet, I'll unarm again.
> Why should I war without the walls of Troy,
> That find such cruel battle here within?
> Each Trojan that is master of his heart
> Let him to field: Troilus, alas, hath none
>
> (I.i.1-5)

and the trope of the procession in the first Cressida scene, I.ii.

In III.iii this tension, outside-inside, is expressed in several ways. For instance, a man cannot know what he has until it is reflected by others. Second, a person with a beautiful face does not know its beauty until it is reflected in the eyes of others. Third, the eye cannot see itself until it is reflected in another eye. Fourth, wit remains unknown until it is expressed. Fifth, if a flint is struck by iron, fire will come forth; thus, fire is inherent in flint:

> *Achilles.* What are you reading?
> *Ulysses.*   A strange fellow here
> Writes me, that man, how dearly ever parted,
> How much in having, or without or in,
> Cannot make boast to have that which he hath,
> Nor feels not what he owes, but by reflection,
> As, when his virtues shining upon others
> Heat them, and they retort that heat again
> To the first giver.
> *Achilles.*   This is not strange, Ulysses.
> The beauty that is borne here in the face
> The bearer knows not, but commends itself
> To others' eyes; nor doth the eye itself,
> That most pure spirit of sense, behold itself,
> Not going from itself; but eye to eye oppos'd
> Salutes each other with each other's form;
> For speculation turns not to itself
> Till it hath travell'd and is mirror'd there
> Where it may see itself. This is not strange at all.
>   (III.iii.94-111)

Speaking of Ajax, Thersites notes,

> Why, a stalks up and down like a peacock, a
> stride and a stand; ruminates like an hostess that
> hath no arithmetic but her brain to set down her
> reckoning; bites his lip with a politic regard, as
> who should say 'There were wit in this head, and
> 'twould out'—and so there is; but it lies as coldly
> in him as fire in flint, which will not show with-
> out knocking.
>   (III.iii.250-57)

By picking up this dominant trope, Shakespeare uses III.iii as an epilogue to the preceding action. The epilogue-like nature of III.iii establishes the design of the play and reinforces the choric function of the scene. It allows Shakespeare to ventilate the preceding difficulties. Troilus, for example, feels the tension in I.i when he states that he cannot fight because of his inner feelings for Cressida. Cressida, on the other hand, comes to the Greek camp in IV.v as an outside element; along with Hector, Cressida symbolically informs the Greek camp with love, although nothing good comes of this. She allows Pandarus to believe that she has no feelings for Troilus; yet she in her soliloquy reveals that her feelings are very strong for him, that inside she feels for Troilus while outside she must remain steadfast. Helen is the outside element to inform the Trojan world. Achilles wishes to stay inside his tent, not engaging in the battles of the war: he wishes to remain in his private world, not submitting to the public demands. And the list can go on.

Thus III.iii, like an epilogue, concludes or ventilates the issues of several scenes: it is like I.i and I.ii in that it uses the Troilus and Cressida tropes of the first two scenes. It is like III.i in that Calchas is in III.iii and Helen is in III.i, the only time in the play that each of these characters appears on stage. Helen is a Greek in Troy; Calchas is a Trojan in "Greece." Helen is a dishonored wife; Calchas is a dishonored father. Both relate to Cressida. For Cressida is no real wife and no safe daughter. Once she gives herself to Troilus, she becomes a kind of wife, and she surrenders her role (as every wife must) of daughter. Thus in Act III Cressida is bracketed by characters that qualify her various roles. This qualification is necessary if we are to understand the difficult situation in which she eventually finds herself. Giving up the roles of both daughter and wife places Cressida in a dangerous state. What role is left to her?

But III.iii is also like II.iii: it is a Greek scene that contains all of the Greek leaders. It naturally follows I.iii, II.i, II.iii; it is in the Greek sequence and the Greek concern is Achilles; here (III.iii) the Greeks confront Achilles. The point is that III.iii is choric because it is a kind of version of these earlier scenes while establishing the character equations.

Clearly, in retrospect, the outside-inside tension relates to and prepares us for Hector's fascination with the sumptuous armor in Act V:

> Stand, stand, thou Greek; thou art a goodly mark.
> No? wilt thou not? I like thy armour well:
> I'll frush it and unlock the rivets all
> But I'll be master of it. Wilt thou not, beast, abide?
> (V.vi.27-30)

Therefore, III.iii not only acts as an epilogue to past action but also functions as a prologue to future action. In Act V Hector will discover that inside the beautiful outer layer is a putrefied core, a rotten center. Shakespeare uses the same tension in Sonnet 146, "Poor soul, the centre of my sinful earth," and in *The Merchant of Venice*. This is a metaphor for both the public and the private plots of the play. What appears to be a noble cause, the retrieving of Helen, is, like Troilus's achievement of Cressida, in reality a selfish event: its center of motivation is rotten. Thus the complications of this trope and tension are implicit in the Act V action. The scene is therefore like a prologue.

The fire in the flint draws our attention to the various elements that are related to this metaphor. The fire will come from the flint only with the knocking: "'There were wit in this head, and 'twould out'—and so there is; but it lies as coldly in him as fire in a flint, which will not show without knocking" (III.iii.254-57). We must relate this comment to Aeneas, who brings fire to the stage in IV.i, and who "kills" Pandarus with his knocking in IV.ii. He comes from the outside in order to inform Troilus of Cressida's impending exchange. Aeneas is another outside element that comes to the Greek camp in I.iii; there he carries Hector's challenge. And in the very next scene, IV.i, Aeneas comes bearing the fire or light, symbolically suggesting that he is a kind of answer, or carries with him a kind of answer, to the difficult circumstances of the conflict and the affair, the answer to both the Trojan and the Greek dilemmas.

That Aeneas plays the role of the outsider alerts us to the strategy of the outsider in terms of other characters. For instance, Cressida and Hector come as outsiders to the Greek camp. If III.i emphasizes love (cupid love), III.iii emphasizes "outside" honor. Cressida and Hector will come to the Greek camp in IV.v. Love, in the form of Cressida, and honor, in the form of Hector, will arrive from the outside in the next major ending, IV.v. Thus the end of Act III prepares us for what we will see at the end of Act IV and qualifies our understanding of what we have seen in the preceding scenes. It is both prologue and epilogue. The end of the first stage of *Troilus and Cressida* presents us with the ideas that will be turned into actions as the play progresses as well as informs the actions that have gone before. It therefore must be read with an eye to both the future and the past.

* * *

Act III.iii opens with Agamemnon and Calchas; it then presents the procession of Greek soldiers who pass by Achilles; Achilles and Ulysses discuss why Achilles has been treated as he has; Thersites enters, and he and Achilles discuss Ajax; Thersites ends with a soliloquy. In terms of the choric import of the scene, it is useful to note that the Greek scene, III.iii, begins with a father-traitor and ends with a bastard. Calchas changes and challenges the nature and the value of the Troilus and Cressida offstage action; Thersites is the fool of war. Calchas's past action of being a traitor affects the present Troilus and Cressida action; Thersites's conclusion that everything is a cuckold and a whore makes a choric remark about the future of Troilus and Cressida.

The general design of III.iii is that of III.i: a prologue; action; an epilogue. In III.iii the prologue is, as we have noted, the meeting between Pandarus and the servant; the central action concerns Pandarus and Paris and Helen; the scene ends with Paris and Helen. In III.iii, on the other hand, the "prologue" is the meeting between Calchas and Agamemnon. As the prologue in III.i gives us a choric context of service with the nameless servant and Pandarus, so the prologue of III.iii presents service of a different kind being rewarded. Calchas notes, "Now, princes, for the service I have done,/Th'advantage of the time prompts me aloud /To call for recompense" (III.iii.1-3). The prologue to the main action of III.i offers service in the context of faith, friendship, grace, praise, the Lord; these pertain to the new lesson of Christian love, love that is the product of betrayal and death. In III.iii the notion of service is presented in the context of recompense, or, to put it another way, commodity. It is a service that demands an immediate reward, a reward for betrayal. It is a concern for only self-interest, the pervasive sin in *Troilus and Cressida*. Calchas wants to be rewarded for his past treacherous acts toward Troy. We may argue that the prologue of III.i thus concerns only love and that the prologue of III.iii concerns only wisdom and power. The love off stage in III.iii is put in the context of wisdom and power, *Greek* concerns on stage. Agamemnon's agreement to grant Calchas's request places the Troilus and Cressida affair in jeopardy, but it also provides Troilus and Cressida and their love a test and a challenge.

Ulysses's speech on time in III.iii extends the thematic concerns of his speech on degree in I.iii; both speeches are vital.[3] As we have noted, III.iii naturally follows and extends I.iii. This is part of the general strategy of III.iii: it is presented as a version of other scenes. And it is important to note that Aeneas enters I.iii after the degree speech and that Aeneas enters at the beginning of Act IV, after the time speech; as we have argued, Aeneas, the true son of Venus, is a key to understanding the play:

> Time hath, my lord, a wallet at his back
> Wherein he puts alms for oblivion,
> A great-siz'd monster of ingratitudes.
> Those scraps are good deeds past, which are devour'd

As fast as they are made, forgot as soon
As done. Perseverance, dear my lord,
Keeps honour bright: to have done is to hang
Quite out of fashion, like a rusty mail
In monumental mockery.

(III.iii.145-53)

and

For Time is like a fashionable host
That slightly shakes his parting guest by th'hand,
And with his arms out-stretch'd, as he would fly,
Grasps in the comer. Welcome ever smiles,
And farewell goes out sighing. O let not virtue seek
Remuneration for the thing it was;
For beauty, wit,
High birth, vigour of bone, desert in service,
Love, friendship, charity, are subjects all
To envious and calumniating Time.

(III.iii.165-74)

We may say that Shakespeare in III.iii emphasizes a time consideration. It is a general choric concern, but it is also a particular concern in terms of the Troilus and Cressida situation. After Troilus and Cressida consummate their vows off stage, time is what they lack, as III.iii demonstrates.

The correlative nature of the scene is clear. In a procession one character *replaces* another, which is first made evident in I.ii, the scene in which Cressida watches the procession of Trojan soldiers. Thersites pageants Ajax. Thersites is Ajax or is a version of him, just as Calchas is Pandarus, as we have indicated. Pandarus has replaced Calchas in Troy. The advice Ulysses is here giving to Achilles is precisely the position that Hector has taken. Thus this "choric" scene not only allows us to consider Ulysses but also allows us to consider Hector. Hector wishes to fight Achilles in order to gain what he has lost, his honor in being defeated by Ajax. He knows, unlike Achilles, that if he does not act quickly he will be forgotten. Hector wants to redeem his lost opinion *now* because it has been lost; importunate, Hector does not want to wait. Time is important to him. Not only are Hector and Ulysses equated but also are Hector and Cressida. Cressida is at this precise moment losing her value. Both Hector and Cressida will lose honor. Hector has issued his challenge; Cressida will have no way of redeeming herself, which she is aware of in her soliloquy in I.ii; Troilus will reject her. Achilles will murder Hector after Hector has killed Patroclus. Thus Shakespeare makes clear the choric nature of III.iii and establishes the character equations.

Achilles is like Troilus: he does not want to fight: he wants to stay at home. On the battlefield love will bring him out of his tent: lost love will bring Achilles forth. It is true that lost love will turn Troilus from love to war. But the point is that both Troilus and Achilles will go from inside to outside; their efforts will be directed outward, from themselves. Like Cressida in I.ii, Achilles decides not to enter the world. And like Cressida, who is presented with a procession in I.ii, Achilles is presented with a procession in III.iii. His position in III.iii is attacked, but he, like Cressida, is unmoved. Thus the "procession" in III.iii is like the procession in I.ii. Ulysses here tries to subvert Achilles in the way that Pandarus in I.ii tries to subvert Cressida.[4] Since, in terms of choric response, Achilles may be equated with Troilus and Cressida, character equation, therefore, becomes a central function of III.iii. The strategy is in fact documented by the pageant of Ajax in the second half of III.iii.

* * *

Act III.ii, the first scene in which Troilus and Cressida are together, is bracketed by III.i and III.iii. As we have seen, III.i provides a context in which we may view the Troilus and Cressida action. But we readily understand the feelings of both Troilus and Cressida as a result of the action at the beginning of III.iii: while Troilus and Cressida are consummating their vows off stage, on stage Calchas is granted his request that Cressida be returned to him. We may see this situation as a test of Troilus's love. This test is articulated in IV.iv when Troilus and Cressida discuss the implications of the notion of being true to each other. If indeed the situation may be seen as a test for Troilus, then he refuses it or fails it. In part he fails because he doesn't hear Cressida's grief, as we have seen. He fumbles Cressida away and fails the test. But then the Trojans, Troilus specifically, have neither wisdom nor power. He comes to doubt her completely, proclaiming that she is only words, "no matter from the heart" (V.iii.108). Our sympathies are with Cressida; Troilus lets her go.

Still, one of the reasons for their failure (for Cressida fails too) is the lack of time, which is in part the reason for Ulysses's choric speech in III.iii. Time is their enemy. As Troilus notes in Act IV:

And suddenly; where injury of chance
Puts back leave-taking, jostles roughly by
All time of pause, rudely beguiles our lips
Of all rejoindure, forcibly prevents
Our lock'd embrasures, strangles our dear vows
Even in the birth of our own labouring breath.
We two, that with so many thousand sighs
Did buy each other, must poorly sell ourselves
With the rude brevity and discharge of one.
Injurious Time now with a robber's haste
Crams his rich thiev'ry up, he knows not how;
As many farewells as be stars in heaven,
With distinct breath and consign'd kisses to them,
He fumbles up into a loose adieu,
And scants us with a single famish'd kiss
Distasted with the salt of broken tears.
                                        (IV.iv.32-47)

In III.iii we see how ineffective wisdom and power are; in III.i we see how ineffective love is. Without time, Troilus and Cressida dissolve. In time Troy itself will fall.

* * *

The main characters in III.iii are Ulysses and Achilles. In terms of the Apple of Discord, Ulysses represents wisdom and Achilles represents power. The two Greek worlds of I.iii (Ulysses-wisdom) and II.i (Achilles-power) meet here in III.iii. And it is, as we might expect, wisdom that attempts to manipulate power. The Greek action reaches a climax here in III.iii. As we have seen, it is part of the Greek sequence of I.iii, II.i, II.iii. The point is that Trojan love has reached a conclusion with the offstage consummation of the affair between Troilus and Cressida; public Greek wisdom and power are here presented on stage. We may see the culmination of the Greek concern (wisdom-power) here since we are *at this moment* (in offstage action) aware of the culmination of the Trojan concern (love).

A central strategy of III.iii, therefore, is offstage correlative action. We know that while Calchas and Agamemnon and Ulysses and Achilles talk on stage in III.iii Troilus and Cressida are off stage consummating their "marriage." Since one episode of III.iii is Thersites pretending to be Ajax, we may suppose that we should imagine one character as being like another, as we have previously established. Character equation, or character replacement, is the thrust of Ulysses's time speech, the same concern as Shakespeare's Sonnet 60:

> Like as the waves make towards the pebbled shore,
> So do our minutes hasten to their end,
> Each changing place with that which goes before,
> In sequent toil all forwards do contend.

$$(1-4)$$

Ulysses, for instance, is like Troilus: he is not being honest with Achilles just as Troilus is not being honest with Cressida; he says he wants Achilles to realize himself, but he doesn't mean it. Ulysses is serving his own ends. We will see the equation of Troilus with Ulysses more fully in IV.v and V.ii. By equation, off stage Troilus is not being honest with Cressida. We see the implications of this equation in IV.iv when Troilus and Cressida question each other's truthfulness. Achilles, like Cressida, knows the truth (see her soliloquy in I.ii) but refuses to believe it. Achilles comments, "I have a woman's longing" (III.iii.236). Ulysses doesn't want Achilles to leave his tent. Achilles doesn't relent or change. Thersites notes that Ajax mistakes him for Agamemnon, an equation that links a bastard and a general. Offstage correlative action directs us to understand the relationship between what we see onstage and what we know is happening away from the stage.

Because Achilles is not on stage throughout, III.iii is not so clearly recapitulative, in terms of a character who remains on stage, as the first two scenes of the play are. But this fact is also true of III.i. Although III.iii is clearly choric, it is also recapitulative. The scene itself, that central portion without the prologue or the epilogue, is, I should like to suggest, the play from the point of view of Achilles. Just as III.i is the play from Pandarus's point of view, as we have demonstrated, so III.iii may be seen as Achilles's scene. Achilles is in II.i and II.iii, but now we get his scene, the scene that presents the problem of the play from his viewpoint. This is a continuation of the strategy employed in the first five scenes. There, as Kenneth Muir has made clear, the play establishes five major viewpoints.[5] The general choric value of III.iii does not diminish the value of it as being the Achilles scene. Act III.iii is a refining of the Greek subplot in terms of Achilles, fusing it with the main plot. The public plot will be resolved when Achilles kills Hector in Act V. The end of Act III, which is the end of an action, fuses the two plots: we get the Achilles "plot" established, but it is qualified by our awareness of the Troilus and Cressida action. We know that Achilles will kill Hector; thus Achilles is unmoved here, as we have noted. Yet in terms of the complexity of the play, the Achilles story, like the Ulysses or the Aeneas story, is important; it isn't, however, emphasized.[6] We can see how the Ulysses action in I.iii frustrates the Hector action in II.ii. Achilles's action here frustrates Greek action.

* * *

Aeneas comes in the next Act as a counter to love in III.ii that is without wisdom and power and as a counter to wisdom and power in III.iii that is without love. He bears the light in the form of a fire: he comes, symbolically, to show us the way. He is a crucial character in the private action of the play (he serves Hector, but he also serves the private plot by appearing in I.i with Troilus and by appearing in IV.ii, IV.iv, and IV.v); he appears at the beginning of the fourth Act with the fire. Aeneas's role is important because, unlike Pandarus, he is the true son of Venus, as we have seen. Unlike Calchas, he is a true man of honor. True love and honor are represented by Aeneas. His light symbolically represents enlightenment and possibility. He speaks of *heavenly business*, *health*, and *human gentleness*. Aeneas is secure because he can submit himself to others. Yet we know that he will betray Dido. Thus the ironies are apparent; Aeneas is limited too. He is serving a vain Hector. The emphasis on time serves to alert us to the future. Therefore, the movement of *Troilus and Cressida* may be described as from Pandarus in III.i and III.ii to Calchas in III.iii to Aeneas in IV.i. The movement is from false love in the form of Pandarus to false honor in the form of Calchas to real love and real honor in the form of Aeneas. In terms of the dramatic action, Aeneas seems to be an answer to Ulysses and Achilles. Eventually, he will leave Troy and its battered walls behind. But only after Ulysses and the Trojans arrive inside the city in the belly of the famous horse. The Trojan horse, therefore, is the most important result of the outside-inside trope; it is the logical and historical extension of the trope and, for an understanding of the play, has the same status as the Apple of Discord.

NOTES

1. Geoffrey Auggeler, "Madness in Reason: A Paradoxical Kinship in *Troilus and Cressida*," *Wascana Review* 9 (1974): 39-57. Although he does not see the relationship

between *Troilus and Cressida* and other plays in precisely the same terms as I do, Auggeler nevertheless sees the play as being very much related to *King Lear, Othello, Macbeth, The Winter's Tale,* and *The Tempest.* See also Jarold W. Ramsey, "The Provenance of *Troilus and Cressida,*" *Shakespeare Quarterly* 21 (1970): 240. Ramsey suggests that we must see *Troilus and Cressida* in the light of the other plays. Otherwise, we cannot hope to define its place among the other, greater contributions that Shakespeare made.

2. See William B. Bache, "Lear as Old Man, Father, King," *CLA Journal* 19 (1975): 1-9.

3. See Frederick Turner, *Shakespeare and the Nature of Time: Moral and Philosophical Themes in Some Plays of William Shakespeare* (Oxford: The Clarendon Press, 1971). See also Ralph Berry, *The Shakespearean Metaphor: Studies in Language and Form* (Totowa: Roman and Littlefield, 1978).

4. "That [Ulysses's] purpose is not to enlighten Achilles about his true identity would be clear to anybody but that conceited and obtuse athlete" (Rolf Soellner, *Shakespeare's Patterns of Self-Knowledge* [Columbus: Ohio Univ. Press, 1972], 196). It is clear that Ulysses is being politically deceptive to an end other than that which he has announced.

5. See n. 1 chap. 3 above.

6. "The motives of Achilles are love, both of Polyxena and Patroclus, and excessive pride" (Kenneth Muir, *Aspects of Shakespeare's 'Problem Plays'* [Cambridge: Cambridge Univ. Press, 1982], 103).

7

The Ulysses Scene

Since for the first and only time in the play the Greeks and the Trojans are together on stage in IV.v, the scene is clearly significant. In Shakespeare's usual practice, the last scene of the fourth Act is the end of an action. It is a step beyond the end of Act III. For instance, IV.iv of *1 Henry IV*, a short scene, is a kind of epilogue to IV.iii. It is very much like and thus reflects the very end of IV.i of *Richard II*, an epilogue episode. If we think of IV.iv of *1 Henry IV* as being part of IV.iii and if, thus, the two scenes together are like IV.i of *Richard II*, we may see the action of IV.iii and IV.iv of *1 Henry IV* as being like IV.v of *Troilus and Cressida*. That is, an enemy enters the enemy's "camp"; in both scenes an "outsider" of primary importance comes to the stronghold of his enemy. In IV.i, the only scene of Act IV of *Richard II*, Richard, the outsider, comes to Henry's court. In IV.iii of *1 Henry IV*, Sir Walter Blunt comes to Hotspur's camp. In IV.v of *Troilus and Cressida*, Cressida and Hector and Troilus come to the Greek camp.

In IV.vii, the last scene of Act IV of *Hamlet*, we hear of Hamlet's return: he now is represented by a messenger (like Blunt) and a letter. Now Hamlet, the enemy of Denmark, has returned to Danish soil. In the scene we are also informed of Ophelia's death. Now that Claudius has enlisted Laertes as the means of destroying Hamlet, a public door is closed; now that Ophelia is dead, a private door is closed. This double action in *Hamlet* of Hamlet's return and then of

Ophelia's death is like the double action in IV.v of *Troilus and Cressida*: Cressida and Hector and Troilus "replace" Hamlet and Ophelia.[1] Because Lear is the king and thus represents Britain, *King Lear* uses the basic pattern differently. In IV.vii of *King Lear*, Lear and Cordelia are reunited. Lear and Cordelia are now enemies of Britain; they have "returned" to the "camp" of the enemy. They, like Hamlet and Ophelia and like Troilus and Cressida, may be said to be in the stronghold of the enemy. In any event, the emphasis is on Hamlet and Ophelia, though they do not appear in IV.vii of *Hamlet*. The emphasis is on Lear and Cordelia in the private world in IV.vii of *King Lear*. In *1 Henry IV*, the play moves to the battlefield in Act V. In *Hamlet*, the play moves to a kind of battlefield in V.ii; in *King Lear*, the play moves to the battlefield in Act V. In all three plays, Act IV is a real but inconclusive end. The procedure is similar in *Troilus and Cressida*.

In IV.v of *Troilus and Cressida*, representatives of Troy come to the Greek camp. In keeping with the Apple of Discord trope, we may say that all of the arrivals can be identified as love or the heart, as persons who feel and are vulnerable. All of the play's major characters appear in IV.v (Agamemnon, Ajax, Achilles, Patroclus, Menelaus, Ulysses, Nestor; Cressida, Hector, Aeneas, Troilus, Paris, Deiphobus, and, according to the Folio, Helenus). Act V in *Hamlet*, *King Lear*, and in *1 Henry IV* ends in death. Except for Prince Harry in *1 Henry IV*, the best are destroyed in Act V. In a sense, this is also true of *Troilus and Cressida*. Those who enter the Greek camp in IV.v, Cressida, Hector, Troilus, will be destroyed in Act V: Hector will be physically destroyed by Achilles and the Myrmidons; Troilus and Cressida will be metaphorically destroyed.

* * *

In III.iii of *Troilus and Cressida*, Shakespeare ventilates or explores a situation that has just reached a point of climax, so, in a sense, IV.v catches up or fuses or condenses both I.iii, the Greek council scene, and II.ii, the Trojan council scene. Just as III.iii draws upon earlier scenes for its significance, so IV.v draws upon earlier scenes. It resolves the essential plot action of these two earlier scenes. Since Pandarus and Thersites are not in I.iii and II.ii, they are not expected and they are not here. Achilles and Ajax appear in IV.v because they are the important plot consideration in both I.iii and II.ii. Act IV.v completes the action begun by Ulysses in I.iii, where the lottery is rigged: in order to subvert Achilles, Ulysses proposes the lottery, by means of which Ajax will replace

Achilles. In II.ii Hector wants the war to continue so that he can redeem the honor he lost when struck down by Ajax. Hector wants to meet and fight Achilles. As we have observed, Ulysses in the Greek council scene of I.iii frustrates and stultifies Hector's plan in the Trojan council scene of II.ii: Hector gets what he wants in II.ii but it is to no avail because of Ulysses's action in I.iii. Now IV.v presents the culmination of that plot action. In this way, IV.v is the end of an action: both Hector and Ulysses are frustrated and stultified. Ajax is as bad as Achilles. Hector's new battle with Ajax is and must be inconclusive, as Hector knows.

In IV.v Cressida says to Menelaus, "You are an odd man" (IV.v.41). This reference to the "odd man" is a joke. But, significantly, this joke seems to refer to a concern for odd and even. At the end of Hector's appearance in IV.v Ajax says to Achilles, "The general state, I fear,/Can scarce entreat you to be odd with him" (IV.v.263-64). The word *odd* is used thirty-two times in all of Shakespeare. It is used five times in *Troilus and Cressida*, and all five occurrences are in IV.v, a fact indicating its importance. As we have indicated, IV.v fuses I.iii, the Greek council scene, and II.ii, the Trojan council scene. In each of these scenes five important characters appear. Listed in the order in which these important characters speak in I.iii and II.ii, the five important characters are Agamemnon, Nestor, Ulysses, Diomedes, Menelaus; in II.ii the five important characters are Priam, Hector, Troilus, Paris, Helenus. The two opposing sides are evenly balanced. We can therefore match Trojans with Greeks, and if we match them according to their positions of importance in I.iii and II.ii, we get the following: Agamemnon and Priam; Nestor and Hector; Ulysses and Troilus; Diomedes and Paris; Menelaus and Helenus. But if we consider the order of the important characters in IV.v as they are presented to Cressida in the kissing episode, which is the utilization of the Cressida trope of the procession, as demonstrated in I.ii, Ulysses's position is lower in the order. If we consider Ulysses's fallen position and compare the lists from I.iii and II.ii with the new list of characters in IV.v, the scene that fuses I.iii and II.ii, the matches change: Agamemnon and Priam; Nestor and Hector; Diomedes and Troilus; Menelaus and Paris; Ulysses and Helenus. Now the forces have come into line; both Troilus and Paris are evenly matched with their proper enemies. The movement to Act V, therefore, has now been prepared for: although Troilus is ready to kill everyone who opposes him, he will go to the battlefield with the intention of killing Diomedes. Paris, who will one day kill Achilles, will fight Menelaus.

Not only in time will Achilles have the Myrmidons "pierce the head" (IV.v.5) of Hector but also in time Troilus will disavow Cressida. In so far as IV.v looks forward to Act V it functions as a kind of prologue. The death of Patroclus in Act

V will bring Achilles into the conflict: the loss of Patroclus will in time bring the conflict to its ugly end. Patroclus will be missed by Achilles as Helen is missed by Menelaus. Thus, Patroclus's death will bring Achilles from his tent just as the abduction of Helen has brought Menelaus and the Greeks to Troy. The loss of a loved one prompts the trouble. Act IV.v functions also like a prologue in that Achilles and Hector meet but do not fight. This meeting presages their meeting in Act V and the murder of Hector.

But IV.v is also a stage in the Troilus-and-Cressida plot action. Cressida comes to the Greek camp as Hector's precursor. With Pandarus's help, Troilus has managed to bring Cressida into the world; in III.ii she loses her value, and this is the result. Just as the honor of Ulysses and Hector is at risk, so is the honor of Cressida. After Cressida exits with Diomedes and after Ulysses declares that Cressida is one of the "daughters of the game" (IV.v.63), everyone responds to Hector's trumpet with "The Trojan's trumpet" (IV.v.64). In this context, Cressida is meant to be seen as Hector's strumpet, as the *Trojan's (s)trumpet* indicates. Both Cressida and Hector compromise with the Greeks by acceding to their demands and succeed only in compromising love and honor.

As we have indicated, IV.v may be seen as a kind of epilogue to the preceding action in that it draws upon what has been presented. The joining of the Greeks and the Trojans culminates the action, and it reintroduces the trope of the procession, which we first get in I.ii, Cressida's scene, and then in III.iii, Achilles's scene. When the Greeks kiss Cressida, they symbolically re-enact the reason for the conflict. As we have seen, Patroclus's comment to Menelaus, "For thus popp'd Paris in his hardiment,/And parted thus you and your argument" (IV.v.28-29), establishes the metaphoric and symbolic nature of the kissing of Cressida by the Greeks: Cressida is another Helen. In this specific sense, this action is an epilogue to the early action of the source or the genesis of the conflict because it re-enacts the abduction of Helen, but now in terms of Cressida.

* * *

Act IV.v is clearly designed. Cressida comes to the Greek camp to join her father; Hector comes to the Greek camp to effect the challenge that Aeneas has delivered. Thus the scene has two main parts: Cressida is the focus of one part; Hector is the focus of the other. Cressida does not greet her father, however, and Hector must have "another battle" with Ajax. The Greeks expect Hector; Cressida enters. Cressida's entrance at this time in IV.v creates a character equation between Cressida and Hector. As we have indicated, Cressida is "Hector's strumpet." We expect Hector and get Cressida. The Cressida case precedes and clarifies the Hector case. The presentation of the Greeks to Cressida (for they introduce themselves to her rather than Diomedes presenting her to them) is like a procession, which, as we have demonstrated, is the initial Cressida trope. But there are two processions in this scene. The second procession occurs when Hector is introduced to the Greeks. Granted the Cressida-Hector equation, this use of the procession trope is not unexpected. Now Hector "perceives" a procession.

Thus in IV.v Cressida and then Hector come to the Greeks: Hector replaces Cressida. Cressida represents love, which the Greeks lack; Hector represents honor, which the Greeks also lack. By now Cressida is devalued love; Hector is devalued honor. Trojan love and honor coming to Greek power and wisdom lead to a kind of compromise. The result is inconclusive. As IV.v makes clear, trouble began when Ulysses and Diomedes came to Troy in the distant past; the trouble will end when Ulysses and Diomedes (inside the Trojan horse) come to Troy in the near future.

In IV.v love comes to wisdom and power. Love does not work. The real answer is for wisdom and power to come to love. Then Troy will and must fall. Once Troy falls, Aeneas, the son of Venus, can be released. This, then, begins the movement to Christian love, a higher form of love, the product of sacrifice, lessons that cannot be known by the Greeks or the Trojans.[2] That knowledge will come in time. Cressida, as devalued love, and Hector, as devalued honor, are hostage to what they desire. Cressida becomes a victim of love; Hector becomes a victim of honor.

When the trumpet sounds for the second time in IV.v, Hector enters. The sure antagonists in the public plot of the play finally meet: Hector, the vain Trojan, and Achilles, the proud Greek. But before Hector meets Achilles, Hector, as the lottery has determined, must fight Ajax, which isn't really a fight at all but a "maiden battle" (IV.v.87). Hector does not want to fight Ajax, for his honor depends on defeating Achilles. "A maiden battle" is, in another sense, precisely what Cressida has been part of.

In this scene, the opposing sides are balanced, as we have indicated. Hector uses Ajax's half-Trojan, half-Greek nature as the excuse for not continuing the battle. By doing this, Hector forestalls Ulysses. By not fighting Ajax, Hector behaves as if he is still the famous, chivalrous knight.[3] We know, however, that Hector is behaving with self-interest; he must fight Achilles in order to regain his honor.[4] It is useful to note that of the eight times the word *knight* or *knights* is used in the play, IV.v contains six of those uses. Here the knights of both armies meet. The action of the introduction of Cressida to the Greeks attests to the choric and chivalric import of the scene; Ulysses says that Cressida is a whore; this is his viewpoint, which, ironically, is not at all chivalric.[5] As Benedick says in *Much Ado About Nothing*, "In a false quarrel there is no true valor" (V.i.120). And Ulysses, as we have seen in I.iii, cannot be trusted.[6] But the point is that they are all false knights.[7]

When she is on stage, Cressida is kissed five times. Hector is introduced to five Greeks: Agamemnon, Menelaus, Nestor, Ulysses, Achilles. As the order of the kissing of Cressida is significant, as we have indicated, so the order of the greeting of Hector is important. Again, Ulysses has lost his position. Each part of the scene demonstrates Ulysses's fall in stature. We may perhaps further say that the order of Hector's greeting of the Greeks represents the general movement of the play in Hector's terms: the play begins with relative security and ends with his being discredited and then, which is in the future, destroyed. Achilles is the last to meet Hector; Achilles, with the aid of the Myrmidons, will end up murdering Hector.

* * *

Since Ulysses is on stage throughout IV.v, the scene, to apply the general strategy identified by Kenneth Muir,[8] may be described as the play in Ulysses's terms. As we have come to expect, we "need" a scene as we proceed from the perspective of each single, major character. For example, III.i is Pandarus's scene; III.iii is Achilles's scene. Although Pandarus, like Achilles, is important earlier in the play, we need, as we proceed, a scene that is from each character's perspective. Act I.iii is the perspective of two characters, Nestor and Ulysses. Now the emphasis is on Ulysses. Just as III.iii, the end of an action, is the play in Achilles's terms, so IV.v, the end of another action, is the play in Ulysses's terms. But, as we have indicated, IV.v also involves the Trojans and the chief members of the subplot, Troilus and Cressida. But they come as an outside force to the enemy stronghold, and they are at the service of the Ulysses perspective. Act IV.v is a public scene without any soliloquies, and we may suppose that Ulysses's speeches about Cressida and Troilus take the place of the soliloquies, found, for instance, in I.i and I.ii, the play in terms of Troilus and Cressida respectively. It is not then remarkable that in IV.v Ulysses passes judgment on both Troilus and Cressida. But it is the judgment of a man who has been discredited. In I.iii Agamemnon speaks of Ulysses as "Prince of Ithaca" (I.iii.70) who, when he speaks gives us "music, wit, and oracle" (I.iii.74), but in the process Agamemnon identifies Ulysses with the rank Thersites:

> Speak, Prince of Ithaca, and be't of less expect
> That matter needless, of importless burden,
> Divide thy lips, than we are confident
> When rank Thersites opes his mastic jaws
> We shall hear music, wit, and oracle.
> (I.iii.70-74)

In I.iii Ulysses is the third to speak; he follows Agamemnon and Nestor. Now he is last.

If we consider IV.v as prologue, we may say that Thersites and Pandarus are added in Act V; they will bring their choric responses in Act V. In this way, Thersites, with his choric responses, functions on the battlefield like Falstaff in Act V of *1 Henry IV*. On the other hand, Pandarus will return right before the battle and right after it. As we have seen, Ulysses provides the choric comment in IV.v. This is the end of the Ulysses public action. Ulysses will provide choric comment to the Troilus-Cressida-Diomedes action. In IV.v Ulysses discredits Cressida and comments on Troilus, but his opinion is of little value: his wisdom and power have been discredited.

Instead of a soliloquy, we get Ulysses's judgment of first Cressida and then Troilus. Now he responds to Cressida's appearance; like Troilus, Ulysses has not seen Cressida's grief in IV.ii and IV.iv; he reports what Aeneas has told him about Troilus, second-hand information. Imagine Ulysses believing an enemy.[9] Ulysses may act the way he does with Cressida because she has just rejected him. He would be the last to receive a kiss, but Cressida says, "claim it when 'tis due" (IV.v.51). His assessment of Cressida is in part due to envy and malice. Instead of belying Achilles, he now attacks Cressida:

> Fie, fie upon her!
> There's language in her eye, her cheek, her lip—
> Nay, her foot speaks; her wanton spirits look out
> At every joint and motive of her body.
> O, these encounterers, so glib of tongue,
> That give accosting welcome ere it comes,
> And wide unclasp the tables of their thoughts
> To every ticklish reader: set them down
> For sluttish spoils of opportunity
> And daughters of the game.
> (IV.v.54-63)

But Ulysses may be as wrong about Troilus as he is about Cressida. Up to this point in the play, Troilus has not demonstrated any of the characteristics that Ulysses describes. Ironically, Troilus *will become* like Hector in Act V, but then Hector will discredit himself there, as he has, in fact, in IV.v. After Troilus turns against Cressida in V.ii, he will become as "vindicative [as] jealous love" (IV.v.107). Indeed, Troilus, because he will fight for private reasons, will become more dangerous, more savage than Hector. "What [Troilus] has he gives" (IV.v.101); that is, he has given Cressida, whom he had, away. Thus Ulysses, by identifying Troilus with Hector, performs a "prologue" or choric function. As Hector will be destroyed and the public or war aspect of the play will come to an end, so Troilus will be metaphorically destroyed, and the private or love aspect of the play will come to an end. Troilus has neither the power nor the wisdom to prevent this destruction:

> The youngest son of Priam, a true knight;
> Not yet mature, yet matchless; firm of word,
> Speaking in deeds, and deedless in his tongue;
> Not soon provok'd, nor, being provok'd, soon calm'd;
> His heart and hand both open and both free;
> For what he has he gives, what thinks he shows,
> Yet gives he not till judgement guide his bounty,
> Nor dignifies an impare thought with breath;
> Manly as Hector, but more dangerous;
> For Hector in his blaze of wrath subscribes
> To tender objects, but he in heat of action
> Is more vindicative than jealous love.
> They call him Troilus, and on him erect
> A second hope as fairly built as Hector.
>
> (IV.v.96-109)

In IV.v Ulysses has been reduced to subplot intrigue. His public intrigue has come to nothing.[10] Now, as the above speeches by Ulysses indicate, he is more concerned with the affairs of Troilus and Cressida, the primary members of the subplot, than he is with Achilles and Ajax and Hector. His choric function has to be corrected by us. It is corrected both by what precedes IV.v and by what follows it.

At the end of IV.v, Troilus, separating himself from the rest of the company, is accompanied by Ulysses. Their conversation serves as a kind of epilogue to the scene. For in private, after the characters who figure in the public conflict exit,

Troilus and Ulysses speak of Cressida and Diomedes, the concerns of Troilus and
the private problem. In IV.v Troilus and Ulysses speak alone; however, in V.ii
Thersites's choric comments are added to these of Troilus and Ulysses.
Qualifying the war discussions of IV.v, therefore, are the love discussions of
Troilus and Ulysses, which, as we know, will turn out to affect the outcome of
the war and which are not yet qualified by the comments of Thersites:

> *Ulysses.* As gentle tell me, of what honour was
> This Cressida in Troy? Had she no lover there
> That wails her absence?
> *Troilus.* O sir, to such as boasting show their scars
> A mock is due. Will you walk on, my lord?
> She was belov'd, she lov'd; she is, and doth;
> But still sweet love is food for fortune's tooth.
>
> (IV.v.286-92)

The scene serves as a kind of mockery of what happens when love is at the
service of power and wisdom, for Cressida deals with the situation as well as she
can. Hector does too. Cressida behaves as she knows she must. Ulysses calls
Cressida a daughter of the game. Ulysses overpraises Troilus. In V.ii Ulysses will
watch Troilus's love being tested. In this sense, Ulysses's concern for Troilus and
Cressida is a prologue to V.ii. When Pandarus leaves Troilus and Cressida alone
in III.ii and when he returns, we hear the line "Will you walk in, my lord"
(III.ii.60,98). Troilus and Cressida are in the dark while their love is declared.
Now, with Troilus and Cressida apart and with Pandarus's efforts thwarted, we
hear, "Will you walk on, my lord?" (IV.v.290) This again alerts us to the choric
idea of walking on the possibilities invoked by the Christian lesson of love, as
determined by III.i and III.ii. This is a perversion of "walking in [the shadow of]
the lord." Instead of walking in the shadow of the lord, which is what Troilus and
Cressida should have done, they are prepared to walk on the lord. As Ulysses
observes in III.iii,

> Or, like a gallant horse fall'n in first rank,
> Lie there for pavement for the abject rear,
> O'er-run and trampled on.
>
> (III.iii.161-63)

In V.iii Troilus is called savage.
Now at the end of IV.v, Ulysses is with Troilus as Pandarus was in the play's
first scene, the Troilus scene. In I.i Pandarus and Troilus discuss Cressida; in

IV.v Ulysses and Troilus discuss Cressida. Ulysses has therefore replaced Pandarus at Troilus's side in the play's private, love plot. Ulysses has become, like Pandarus, a fool. Act IV.v is a version of I.i. Troilus is still concerned with matters of the heart: "But still sweet love is food for fortune's tooth" (IV.v.292).

* * *

Although, in symbolic terms, love, wisdom and power are on stage in IV.v, they are devalued. If the Greeks and the Trojans were to gain what the other lacks (valued love and valued wisdom and power), the conflict might be satisfied, but, of course, this is not to be. For when Cressida comes to the Greek camp in IV.v, she is abused by Ulysses, unrecognized as the symbolic answer of love. When Hector comes to the Greek camp he fails to see the necessity for power and wisdom; he is blinded by vanity; he has no choice but not to fight Ajax. But like Cressida, he does what he must. As we learn from Ulysses, Troilus is a second Hector. He, too, as we will see in Act V, will become self-absorbed; his concern will turn from love to war; his self-interest will lead to the battlefield and his fruitless revenge.

NOTES

1. Ulysses, says Honor Matthews, "is not himself a lord in any ordered hierarchy. He is a crafty 'dog-fox' who, like Polonius, would 'by indirections find directions out'. He works by fomenting the very factiousness he decries, for he plays off Ajax against Achilles, and Achilles against Ajax, while he inflames the vanity of his leaders as skillfully as he does that of their followers" (*Character and Symbol in Shakespeare's Plays: A Study of Certain Christian Elements in Their Structures* [Cambridge: Harvard Univ. Press, 1962], 105). He sees the similarity between *Troilus and Cressida* and *Hamlet* in Ulysses and Polonius.

2. David Kaula discusses the Christian implications of the text: "If this emphasis on the religious elements in *Troilus* seems to result in an unwarranted 'theologizing' of a play obviously pagan in its setting, the answer is that Shakespeare would hardly have been the first Renaissance writer to interpret a classical fable from a Christian viewpoint" ("'Mad Idolatry' in Shakespeare's *Troilus and Cressida*," *Texas Studies in Literature and Language* 15 [1973]: 37-38).

3. For a discussion of Hector's role as a knight derived from the Medieval tradition of chivalry, see Robert Kimbrough, *Shakespeare's Troilus and Cressida and Its Setting* (Cambridge: Harvard Univ. Press, 1964), 112. Although I agree with Kimbrough that

Hector's character is influenced by this tradition, I cannot agree that Hector is "a perfect knight." Loyalty, temperance, and courage are qualified and undercut by Hector's vanity.

4. What Hector fails to understand is that the age of chivalry is dead. See Kenneth Muir, *Aspects of Shakespeare's 'Problem Plays': Articles Reprinted from Shakespeare Survey* (Cambridge: Cambridge Univ. Press, 1982), 102.

5. "The most superficial reading of *Troilus and Cressida* shows that its manners are those of medieval chivalry and chivalric love, as the Elizabethans understood them" (William W. Lawrence, *Shakespeare's Problem Comedies* [New York: Fredrick Ungar Publishing Co., 1960], 142).

6. "Ulysses may be the cleverest man on stage, but it is by no means certain that Shakespeare meant the spectators to like him. It is probable that Shakespeare was deliberately executing the same surprising inversion of a classical reputation that he elsewhere executed with Caesar and, for a brief flash, with Cicero" (Herbert Howarth, *The Tiger's Heart: Eight Essays on Shakespeare* [New York: Oxford Univ. Press, 1970], 176). This inversion is clearly evident in the light of the how Shakespeare treats this famous character.

7. That the important characters in IV.v are all false knights is, or should be, obvious. Agamemnon's speeches in I.iii have the character of a chivalrous oration. His comments in I.iii alert us to the false nature of the knights in this play when we see them in the context of the impotence of the behavior of the Greeks. As Carolyn Asp notes, "In this play, the knightly love of the courtly tradition is exhibited as a debilitating and illusion-producing enslavement" ("The Expense of Spirit in a Waste of Shame," *Shakespeare Quarterly* 22 [1971], 357).

8. See n. 1 chap. 3 above.

9. That Ulysses would believe Aeneas here is as doubtful as Hamlet's believing the Captain in IV.iv of *Hamlet*. Aeneas is as much an enemy of Ulysses as the Captain is of Hamlet.

10. As William Blisset remarks, Ulysses's lottery "comes to nothing, and Achilles is moved to join the battle not by elaborate secret manoeuvers but by the death of Patroclus and that only" (William Blisset, "Paradox and Ambiguity in *Troilus and Cressida*, *Wascana Review* 9 [1974], 10).

8

The Hector-Troilus Scene

The last scene before the battlefield, V.iii of *Troilus and Cressida*, shares several features with V.ii of *1 Henry IV*, the last scene before the battlefield in that play. In V.ii of *1 Henry IV*, Worcester and Vernon have information that would affect the impending battle: the king has offered to forgive the rebels, but Worcester and Vernon do not tell Hotspur. The battle need not be fought; the destruction need not occur. In *Troilus and Cressida*, on the other hand, Pandarus enters with a letter from Cressida that could affect Troilus's action. Troilus rejects her love and turns to the battlefield and death. But on a deeper level, even if Hotspur were offered safety, he would reject it. Hector and Troilus are worse than Hotspur: they do not listen to reason; they insist on fighting. They put their personal concerns above the concerns of Troy.

In V.iii of *Troilus and Cressida*, two possible, pre-emptive endings are dramatized: the Hector end; the Troilus end. The scene seems meant to be read from a dual perspective: from Hector's perspective with an epilogue (Troilus and Pandarus); from Troilus's perspective with a prologue (Hector and Andromache and Cassandra). Act V.iii is thus the play from both Hector's perspective and Troilus's perspective. From Hector's perspective the end is an epilogue, but from Troilus's perspective it is an end. From Troilus's perspective the beginning is a prologue, but from Hector's perspective it is a beginning. Troilus, who will continue to fight after Hector's death, is another Hector here and on the battlefield. In IV.v Troilus is spoken of by Ulysses as a second Hector, his replacement. The center of the scene is, as we might expect, an obligatory confrontation between the "honorable" Hector and the loveless Troilus. For what Shakespeare does in V.iii is a refinement of the strategy identified by Kenneth Muir and utilized by this discussion.[1] It employs the choric strategy of the prologue and the epilogue in the service of the Muir strategy of shifting viewpoints.

The scene begins with Andromache and Cassandra attempting to convince Hector not to go to battle: they know, as we do, that he will be killed. The scene ends with Troilus rejecting the heart-felt letter from Cressida: rejecting the heart, Troilus doesn't care whether he lives or dies. Troilus confronts Hector while Cassandra is off stage fetching Priam. When Priam and Cassandra "return," they ignore Troilus: their preoccupation is to prevent Hector from going to war. They have not heard the interchange between Troilus and Hector and, thus, do not know that Troilus has made it ironically imperative for Hector to go forth. Hector cannot let Troilus go forth and steal his honor. Hector cannot let Troilus become *the* hero. On a thematic level, we seem meant to see Priam as Trojan power and Cassandra as Trojan wisdom.[2] Greek wisdom and power have been transmuted into ineffective Trojan wisdom and power. They are ineffective against Hector's perverted honor and Troilus's reckless despair. The Apple of Discord is thus transmuted and applied in Trojan terms. Priam and Cassandra are off stage during the confrontation because power and wisdom are meaningless to Hector, who is obsessed with frustrated honor, and Troilus, who is obsessed with frustrated love.[3]

In V.iii only members of the Trojan family are present. Paris and Helen are notably absent. Act V.iii may be said to be a version of II.ii with Paris and Helenus, Trojan love and wisdom, absent. Helen, the cause of Trojan family discord, is expectedly absent. Act II.ii, the Trojan council scene, is the public debate over the war question; V.iii, the Trojan family scene, is a private debate over Hector's going to battle. We may thus say that V.iii is a "revision" of II.ii. Cassandra is in V.iii but is still ineffective. Andromache, the wife, is new. Hector controlled the debate in II.ii so that he could meet Achilles and regain his lost honor. But his end has already been frustrated in I.iii by Ulysses and Nestor.

Because of the action in IV.v, Hector must go to the battlefield, if he is to meet Achilles. Hector was political in II.ii; he is importunate now. But we know that Achilles has decided (V.i) not to go to the battlefield. In this regard, Hector is like Achilles in III.iii. What Achilles does in III.iii and IV.v is to "forestall" and to frustrate Hector's action in V.iii. Hector is going out for honor, but Achilles will not fight. Hector thinks that he can meet Achilles, but, as V.i demonstrates,

Achilles, responding to a major vow, will listen to Hecuba and will not fight. Hector is also like Ulysses in IV.v: there Ulysses is discredited; here, in V.iii, Hector is discredited. The point is that since Troilus must kill (he is like Hector in II.ii), he serves Hector's wish to get what he wants. But by serving his own ends, Troilus is really reinforcing Hector's resolve. We do not know that, after V.iii, Achilles will violate his vow to Hecuba and enter the battlefield.

* * *

Act V.iii is the play from Hector's perspective with a Troilus epilogue just as III.i is the play from Pandarus's perspective with a Paris-and-Helen epilogue, where Helen is asked by Paris to unarm Hector. Hector doesn't hear the epilogue of V.iii just as Troilus doesn't hear the prologue. Act III.iii is the play in Achilles's terms with a prologue by Agamemnon and Calchas and with an epilogue by Thersites. Act V.iii is the play from Troilus's perspective with a prologue by Hector, Andromache, and Cassandra. Hector rejects Andromache, and we see what happens. Unlike Hector, Troilus doesn't have a wife; he ends up rejecting his frail "mistress." The way that Hector begins is played off against Troilus's end: Hector's self-centered honor is played off against Troilus's self-centered revenge. Hector and Troilus exemplify the Trojan parable of honor and love devoid of wisdom and power. In I.ii we hear of Hector's insistence, because of his upset at being defeated by Ajax, on fighting; in V.iii Troilus insists on going forth to the battlefield. Thus, we may see Hector and Troilus as counterparts or doubles.[4]

Again, the scene opens with Andromache and Cassandra attempting to dissuade Hector from entering the battle. Priam's wisdom is to no avail. Hector argues that,

> I am today i'th'vein of chivalry:
> Let grow thy sinews till their knots be strong
> And tempt not yet the brushes of the war.
> Unarm thee, go; and doubt thou not, brave boy,
> I'll stand today for thee and me and Troy.
> (V.iii.32-36)

But no matter how heightened the rhetoric, Hector wants to regain on the battlefield his lost, sullied honor. Troilus will be a new Hector, bloody and vengeful, because he rejects love. Hector, who needs to have Troilus unarmed, resorts, as in II.ii, to politics: he hides his vulgar honor behind the screen of chivalry. Troilus will fight for his private revenge. Troy is deliberately sacrificed by these two heroes, to Hector's lost honor and to Troilus's rejected love.

Troilus doesn't care what anyone else thinks or feels; he wants to kill Diomedes:

> *Troilus.* For th'love of all the gods,
>   Let's leave the hermit pity with our mother;
>   And when we have our armours buckled on
>   The venom'd vengeance ride upon our swords,
>   Spur them to ruthful work, rein them from ruth!
> *Hector.* Fie, savage, fie.
> *Troilus.*   Hector, then 'tis wars.
> *Hector.* Troilus, I would not have you fight today.
> *Troilus.* Who should withhold me?
>   Not fate, obedience, nor the hand of Mars
>   Beckoning with fiery truncheon my retire;
>   Not Priamus and Hecuba on knees,
>   Their eyes o'er-galled with recourse of tears;
>   Nor you, my brother, with your true sword drawn,
>   Oppos'd to hinder me, should stop my way,
>   But by my ruin.
>
>   (V.iii.44-58)

In I.i Aeneas comes on stage to take Troilus to battle; in V.iii Troilus comes on stage "to take" Hector to battle. A love-sick boy in I.i, Troilus cares only about Cressida. He is ready to sacrifice battlefield honor to selfish concerns, to love. In I.i Aeneas appears after the alarm and takes Troilus to battle; in V.iii Hector uses Aeneas's presence on the battlefield as part of his argument to go forward. Aeneas; then Hector; then Troilus. Because Aeneas ultimately will lead toward Rome and the Christian lesson of love, following him would provide a metaphoric answer. But Aeneas is not here; he is on the battlefield.

During the central confrontation with Hector in V.iii Troilus says, "Spur them to ruthful work, rein them from ruth" (V.iii.48). This comment shows Troilus's disregard for ruth, pity. Hector's response is "Fie, savage, fie" (V.iii.49). But since we are concerned with the answer provided by women in the scene (Andromache, Cassandra, Cressida), but not accepted by either Hector or Troilus, we perhaps should see *ruth* as the biblical Ruth, the Old Testament figure of faithful service. Helen and Cressida, unfaithful women, are not on stage. Troilus rejects pity and then Cressida and love. In V.ii Troilus stops his ears to her "appeal"; now in V.iii he refuses to accept or to see her appeal. The first thing we hear about Hector in I.ii is that he "chid Andromache" (I.ii.6). Here (V.iii) we see him chiding her. There Hector wanted a chivalric test; now he wants justification on the battlefield. Hector is now (V.iii) worse than the way he was then (I.ii). Troilus too has significantly changed: he now wants war and death. As a Trojan family scene (like II.ii), V.iii is a kind of a prologue. Cassandra's last words,[5] "Hector's dead" (V.iii.87) will be echoed in V.ix and V.x:

> O, farewell, dear Hector.
> Look how thou diest: look how thy eye turns pale:
> Look how thy wounds do bleed at many vents;
> Hark how Troy roars, how Hecuba cries out,
> How poor Andromache shrills her dolours forth;
> Behold! distraction, frenzy, and amazement
> Like witless antics one another meet,
> And all cry 'Hector! Hector's dead! O, Hector!'
>   (V.iii.80-87)

To this speech Troilus cries, "Away, away!" (V.iii.88) Thus we are meant to see Cassandra's prediction as an answer, *a way*. Ironically, Hector's death will be a way—out of the fall of Troy—for power and wisdom to come to love. The false love of V.iii must be destroyed or must destroy itself. Ironically, Hector will find not that the gods stand about him but that he will be encompassed by the Myrmidons, who at Achilles's order will butcher him. Hector's death is the price of a future way. Sacrifice and betrayal constitute the way that *the King* will come.[6]

* * *

It is interesting that the epilogue to V.iii echoes and mirrors an episode from V.i. In V.i Thersites delivers a letter from Hecuba to Achilles. While Achilles silently reads the letter, Thersites and Patroclus trade insults. When he completes reading the letter, Achilles comments:

> My sweet Patroclus, I am thwarted quite
> From my great purpose in tomorrow's battle.
> Here is a letter from Queen Hecuba,
> A token from her daughter, my fair love,

Both taxing me, and gaging me to keep
An oath that I have sworn. I will not break it.
Fall, Greeks: fail, fame: honour, or go or stay;
My major vow lies here, this I'll obey.
Come, come, Thersites, help to trim my tent;
This night in banqueting must all be spent.
Away, Patroclus!

(V.i.36-46)

When Pandarus enters with a letter from Cressida for Troilus V.iii ends. This epilogue represents an end of the Troilus-Cressida action, an end of the Troilus-Cressida affair, which will reach its final end in V.x. The end of V.iii is the end of the scene from Troilus's perspective: after this, Troilus can have no wife. The scene begins with Hector rejecting his wife; the scene ends with Troilus rejecting the person who should have been his wife. Now Troilus, rather than the Hector of the prologue, rejects an appeal from the heart. The effect of the letter is the opposite of its intention. It is a moment when a Troilus end is offered, but it is too late for Troilus to change. The characters involved in the V.i and V.iii actions mirror each other: Achilles is like Troilus; Thersites and Patroclus are like Pandarus.

After Troilus reads the letter, he tears it up. In I.ii Cressida's soliloquy begins with a list: "Words, vows, gifts, tears, and love's full sacrifice" (I.II.287). Here Troilus's comment begins with "Words, words, mere words, no matter from the heart" (V.iii.108). Whereas Cressida's list implies that her movement in the play is from words to "love's full sacrifice,"[7] Troilus's movement is from love to "words, mere words." For Troilus, Cressida, the heart, has lost her value:

Words, words, mere words, no matter from the heart;
Th'effect doth operate another way.
Go, wind, to wind: there turn and change together.
My love with words and errors still she feeds,
But edifies another with her deeds.

(V.iii.108-12)

The point is that the Achilles-Patroclus-Thersites episode in V.i may be seen as a kind of a prologue to the Trojan action both in V.ii and V.iii; the end of V.iii is an epilogue to that same action. We know, as we have previously determined, that Achilles's action (V.i) forestalls Hector's desire to meet and kill Achilles on

the battlefield. We know the Hector-Achilles connection. We now get a
Troilus-Achilles connection.

In V.i Thersites brings a letter to Achilles, which is an action like this one in
V.iii. On the one hand, Thersites, the Greek fool of war, brings the letter in V.i;
on the other hand, Pandarus, the Trojan fool of love, brings the letter in V.iii.
In V.i the result of the letter to Achilles is to make Achilles remember his vow
not to fight for love's sake: he responds to Hecuba, the mother not in V.iii; in
V.iii the result of the letter to Troilus is that Troilus disregards his vows to
Cressida. He gives in to the "higher" course of revenge. Troilus and Achilles are
in similar positions in these scenes; each acts differently to a letter; each reacts
differently. Troilus doesn't listen to Cressida; Achilles does listen to Hecuba. The
Achilles action in V.i glosses the Troilus action in V.iii.

While Achilles reads the letter in V.i, the slanderous argument between
Thersites and Patroclus occurs; while Troilus reads the letter in V.iii, Pandarus
coughs and complains about his sickness. This is onstage correlative action. The
slander *on stage* in V.i relates to the Greeks (or to the war), and the complaining
on stage in V.iii relates to the Trojans (or to love): Cressida will become a leper.
In part the reason for Troilus's reaction is his eavesdropping scene in V.ii; he has
just seen Cressida with Diomedes. But, more important, Troilus, as a Trojan, has
no power and wisdom. He now has only frustrated love, and his reaction is in
part based on this fact. Achilles, as a Greek, has no real love; he has only power
and wisdom, although he will respond to love when Hector kills Patroclus. Thus
Achilles can abide by a higher vow; Troilus serves a lesser vow. Hector in V.iii
is like Achilles in III.iii, and Troilus in V.iii is like Achilles in V.i. The onstage
correlative action demonstrates that in V.i Thersites and Patroclus are like
Pandarus in V.iii; Thersites and Patroclus are "replaced" by Pandarus. The ugly
talk of Thersites and Patroclus is balanced by Pandarus's cough in V.iii. The
Achilles episode in V.i is like a prologue to the Troilus epilogue of V.iii: Achilles
won't go to battle; Troilus will go to battle. Pandarus is rejected here as Thersites
will be rejected on the battlefield. These Greeks are like this Trojan: wisdom and
power are like love. As Troilus silently reads the letter to himself, Pandarus
coughs:

> A whoreson tisick, a whoreson rascally tisick, so
> troubles me, and the foolish fortune of this girl,
> and what one thing, what another, that I shall
> leave you one o'th's days; and I have a rheum in
> mine eyes, too, and such an ache in my bones that

unless a man were cursed I cannot tell what to
think on't. What says she there?

(V.iii.101-07)

Under these circumstances, all are ineffective. Ultimately, Achilles will go to the battlefield.

Troilus's speech in V.iii ends with a disregard for heart-felt words and a determination to produce bloody deeds. He does not believe the words of the girl to whom he has given his heart; he believes only her deeds, as he understands them. Cressida does not see Troilus in V.ii. Cressida behaves as she does with Diomedes there and with Troilus here because she is trapped. Whatever action she takes is in part conditioned by the circumstances in which she finds herself. Troilus, who is prompted to believe only what he sees by the loveless Ulysses, is both disregarding Cressida's words in the letter, and, more important, forgetting the vows exchanged between them in IV.iv. Because Troilus has witnessed V.ii, the "wisdom" and the "power" of the Greeks have destroyed his love. For Troilus the battle is now a matter of winning or losing: "I come to lose my arm, or win my sleeve" (V.iii.96). For Troilus, no end other than killing is possible.

NOTES

1. See n. 1 chap. 3 above.

2. See Harold Goddard, *The Meaning of Shakespeare* 2 vols. (Chicago: The Univ. of Chicago Press, 1951), 2: 33. Harold Goddard considers Priam to be the symbolic agent of wisdom in the play.

3. "Time proves how finite are the love and honor of Troy" (Frederick Turner, *Shakespeare and the Nature of Time* [Oxford: The Clarendon Press, 1971], 127). This is a good discussion of love and honor in the play.

4. It seems clear that several characters serve as doubles in *Troilus and Cressida*. We may speak of Troilus and Diomedes as counterparts; of Hector and Achilles; of Priam and Agamemnon; of Cressida and Helen; of Pandarus and Thersites. But we may also see doubling as a strategy for design in the play. Clearly I.i and I.ii as well as I.iii and II.ii are meant to be seen as counterparts. Other double actions in the play include the letters in V.i and V.iii and the unarming of Hector as a subject in III.i and V.iii.

5. "In the last distracted and frenzied moments of the play . . . Cassandra's phrase 'Hector's dead!' is repeated eight times in less than forty lines. . . . [this] emphatically validates Cassandra's vision of the ensuing ruin and establishes beyond doubt her role in the formal and visionary structure of the play" (Richard D. Fly, "Cassandra and the

Language of Prophecy in *Troilus and Cressida*," *Shakespeare Quarterly* 26 [1975]: 161).

6. At the beginning of Act V of *Richard II* the Queen says, "This way the King will come" (V.i.1). Although she waits on Richard, the end of IV.i suggests that the king is Christ: "I'll lay/A plot shall show us a merry day" (IV.i.333-34). In *Troilus and Cressida*, Hector's death will result in the destruction of Troy. This will enable Aeneas to lead to Rome and through Rome to point the way to the coming of Christ. Hector is the sacrifice that must be paid before Troy can fall and *the* King can come.

7. "The poignance of [Cressida's] situation at the end of the play is emphasized by Troilus's dismissal of that whose vestiges prompt her to try to reach him with what he disdainfully calls 'words, words, mere words; no matter from the heart' (V.iii.109)" (Carolyn Asp, "In Defense of Cressida," *Studies in Philology* 74 [1977]: 417). I must agree with Asp.

9

Thersites and the Battlefield Scenes

When the setting of *Troilus and Cressida* is the battlefield, Thersites functions as a character who comments about both the Greeks and the Trojans.[1] He appears in only two scenes, V.iv and V.vii, where in thirty-nine lines Thersites twice comments about onstage action, has two confrontations, and delivers two soliloquies.[2] It is not unusual for Shakespeare to use a character to comment on battlefield action. In *1 Henry IV*, for instance, Falstaff functions in a comparable way. Like Thersites in *Troilus and Cressida* who has two soliloquies on the battlefield, Falstaff has five soliloquies, two comments about onstage action, and three confrontations. Like Falstaff in Act V of *1 Henry IV*, Thersites in Act V of *Troilus and Cressida* qualifies the action of this play and helps us to understand its significance.

Thersites both begins and ends V.iv with a soliloquy. Since Thersites is on stage throughout V.iv, and since V.iv contains Thersites's two soliloquies, this scene may be considered the play from his perspective.[3] Moreover, his soliloquies bracket the action in the scene, like a kind of prologue and epilogue. Troilus and Diomedes enter and exit fighting: Hector has a brief encounter with Thersites. The scene thus contains the three Thersites battlefield functions: a soliloquy, a comment on action, a confrontation. The scene miniaturizes the Thersites function on the battlefield. As III.i is the play in terms of Pandarus, the fool of love, who is with the good servant and then with Paris and Helen, so V.iv is the play in terms of Thersites, the fool of war, who comments on the major figures of V.iii, Troilus and Hector. We now see Troilus confronting Diomedes, an episode that naturally follows Troilus's rejection of Cressida. Thus V.iv extends V.iii: Troilus and Hector have arrived to the battlefield.

But the essential point is that V.iv is the play from the Thersites perspective, as III.i is the play from the Pandarus perspective. The concern at the end of III.i is Hector: Paris and Helen discuss the unarming of the warrior. At the end of V.iv Hector enters the battlefield and confronts Thersites. Now instead of Pandarus and the good servant, who are in III.i, we get a vicious Thersites; instead of a safe Paris and Helen, we get a vicious Troilus fighting Diomedes; instead of music, we get discord.

This is Thersites's first choric soliloquy:

> Now they are clapper-clawing one another, I'll
> go look on. That dissembling abominable varlet
> Diomed has got that same scurvy, doting, foolish
> knave's sleeve of Troy there in his helm. I would
> fain see them meet, that that same young Trojan
> ass, that loves the whore there, might send that
> Greekish whoremasterly villain with the sleeve
> back to the dissembling luxurious drab of a sleeve-
> less errand. O'th'other side, the policy of those crafty
> swearing rascals—that stale old mouse-eaten dry
> cheese Nestor, and that same dog-fox Ulysses—is
> not proved worth a blackberry. They set me up in
> policy that mongrel cur Ajax, against that dog of
> as bad a kind Achilles, and now is the cur Ajax
> prouder than the cur Achilles, and will not arm
> today; whereupon the Grecians begin to proclaim
> barbarism, and policy grows into an ill opinion.
> (V.iv.1-17)

After being confronted by Hector, Thersites ends V.iv with his second soliloquy:

> God-a-mercy that thou wilt believe me, but a
> plague break thy neck for frighting me.—What's
> become of the wenching rogues? I think they have

swallowed one another. I would laugh at that mir-
acle; yet in a sort lechery eats itself. I'll seek them.

(V.iv.31-35)

Thersites's final appearance in the play is in V.vii. In this scene Thersites
watches Menelaus and Paris fight and meets Margarelon. The Thersites action in
V.vii mirrors the his action in V.iv. While Menelaus and Paris are fighting,
Thersites comments on the action. The meeting between Menelaus and Paris in
V.vii echoes the Troilus-Diomedes meeting in IV.iv, when Diomedes comes to
fetch Cressida, as well as the Hector-Thersites meeting in V.iv, when Thersites
discredits himself with "I am a rascal, a scurvy railing knave" (V.iv.28). Thus
these meetings are a version or an extension of the "meetings" in V.iv. The terms
Thersites uses as he comments on the action are those of the hunt. He sees
Menelaus and Paris as cuckold and cuckold-maker. That he uses the terms of the
hunt is significant because Hector leaves the stage in V.vi chasing the one in
sumptuous armor with the words, "I'll hunt thee for thy hide" (V.vi.31).
Thersites's comments refer, therefore, not only to the combat between Menelaus
and Paris but also to the offstage combat between Hector and the nameless Greek
wearing the beautiful armor. Act V.vii, therefore, gives us the prominent,
identifiable, offstage correlative action, which compares to the Troilus-Diomedes
action in V.iv:

> The cuckold and the cuckold-maker are at it.
> Now, bull! Now, dog! 'Loo, Paris, 'loo!—Now,
> my double-horned Spartan! 'Loo, Paris, 'loo! The
> bull has the game: ware horns, ho![4]

(V.vii.9-12)

Mirroring his meeting with Hector in V.iv, Thersites meets Margarelon in
V.vii. In this meeting, Thersites is both discredited, as we have seen, and the
infection of self-interest in the society is revealed. That he discredits himself is
the significant point about Thersites in V.vii, for now we can see clearly why we
must call his judgment into question. In V.iv Thersites calls himself a rascal, a
knave, a rogue; here he calls himself a bastard. But Margarelon, a new character,
Priam's bastard son, enters and by entering demonstrates that even Priam, the
Trojan head of state, has been infected with the sin of adultery. Now we see how
deeply flawed the Trojan royal family is. Margarelon's entrance adds a new,
unexpected member to the Trojan royal family. He is a bastard, but, strangely,
he can still fight for an ignoble cause. As the comparable design of the V.iv and

V.vii prove, Margarelon is a double for Hector. Thersites is the constant: he is the person who "measures" the others. Troilus and Diomedes are doubles for Paris and Menelaus. We have already seen how the mirroring episodes of V.i and V.iii insist on the identification of Achilles and Troilus. The entrance of Margarelon here is like the use of the letters in V.i and V.iii: Margarelon's presence here establishes the double with Hector as the letters establish the doubles between Achilles and Troilus there. Thersites's last speech shows the depth of the problem:

> I am a bastard, too: I love bastards. I am
> bastard begot, bastard instructed, bastard in
> mind, bastard in valour, in everything illegitimate.
> One bear will not bite another, and wherefore
> should one bastard? Take heed: the quarrel's most
> ominous to us—if the son of a whore fight for a
> whore, he tempts judgement. Farewell, bastard.
>
> (V.vii.16-22)

Thus, in terms of Thersites on the battlefield, there are two prominent confrontations: Thersites confronts Hector in V.iv; Thersites confronts Margarelon in V.vii. In both instances Thersites labels himself. The second battlefield confrontation stills the voice of Thersites in the play; after this confrontation, Thersites disappears. On the battlefield, what Thersites represents, the cynical voice of war and self-interest, is made mute.[5]

* * *

Except for the interlude with Thersites, Hector is in only two battlefield scenes: V.vi and V.viii. In effect, V.vi is a prologue to V.vii; V.viii is an epilogue to V.vii. Act V.vii separates V.vi and V.viii, the two battlefield scenes in which Hector appears. The intervening scene occurs while the offstage action of the battle goes on. In addition to the prologue-epilogue strategy, offstage correlative action is a key strategy in these scenes. It is important for qualifying the Hector action in Act V. While Hector is pursuing the Greek for his armor, there are three kinds of onstage action. We may thus consider the onstage action as being choric.[6]

This strategy may be seen clearly in the relationship between V.vi, V.vii, and

V.viii. At the end of V.vi, Hector chases after the Greek in sumptuous armor. When he returns in V.viii, the scene in which Achilles murders Hector, Hector has a soliloquy and disarms himself. After killing the Greek for the armor, Hector discovers that the body within the armor is a putrefied core:

> Most putrefied core, so fair without,
> Thy goodly armour thus hath cost thy life.
> Now is my day's work done: I'll take my breath.
> Rest, sword; thou hast thy fill of blood and death.
>
> (V.viii.1-4)

Hector is then murdered: because he expended himself for valuable armor, he has "wasted" himself and is vulnerable. The essential trope is that of the caskets in *The Merchant of Venice*, particularly the gold casket that contains "A carrion Death" (II.vii.63). Perhaps the clearest statement of what we may call the outside-inside trope is Sonnet 146:

> Poor soul, the centre of my sinful earth,
> [. . . .] these rebel pow'rs that thee array,
> Why dost thou pine within and suffer dearth,
> Painting thy outward walls so costly gay?
> Why so large cost, having so short a lease,
> Dost thou upon thy fading mansion spend?
> Shall worms, inheritors of this excess,
> Eat up thy charge? Is this thy body's end?
> Then, soul, live thou upon thy servant's loss,
> And let that pine to aggravate thy store;
> Buy terms divine in selling hours of dross;
> Within be fed, without be rich no more:
>   So shalt thou feed on Death, that feeds on men,
>   And Death once dead, there's no more dying then.

We may designate the tension as the soul within the body.

That Margarelon enters in V.vii is important because it is clarified by the offstage correlative action and makes clear the implications of the outside-inside trope. Margarelon is the bastard son of Priam. Priam's infidelity is made plain in this scene. That Hector is off stage fighting for the armor is an indication of how meaningless the Trojan society really is. Hector is concerned with honor. He discovers that it covers corruption, a putrefied core. Margarelon, the bastard son of Priam, is like the putrefied core. With his appearance, we see the "inside" of the Trojan royal family. We see how deeply the disease of infidelity runs in Troy. Although Margarelon's outside is putrefied, his soul is not corrupt. Hector's pursuit of the sumptuous armor reveals his vanity and concern for himself; the appearance of Margarelon indicates the depth of self-interest in the play; it reveals the vanity and self-concern even of the head of state, Priam. For not only are Thersites and Margarelon, the two bastards, motivated by self-interest but also are Priam, Hector, Paris, and Troilus, the male members of the royal family. Margarelon shows us the rottenness of the "good" Trojan family. Like Hector, Margarelon can fight for an ignoble cause. Thus, we may perhaps see the scene as the play from Hector's perspective without Hector on stage. Act V.vii is bracketed by the encompassing Hector action and thus serves to exploit the central tension. The Hector actions in V.vi and V.viii are the prologue and the epilogue to the action of V.vii. This is a further refinement of the Muir strategy, which demonstrates the complexity of the play through shifting perspectives.[7]

We now see Thersites as a bastard: he too is a liar, an outcast of society, the son of a whore. Likewise, Menelaus is revealed as a bull; Paris a dog; Achilles a murderer. Because V.vii is choric, we see the real Achilles, the real Menelaus and Paris, the real Thersites. All are exposed. The war is the outside; Menelaus's "grief and despair" and Paris's "desire" are the inside. Thus the strategy is like the "eye of love" in *Much Ado About Nothing*, or V.iv and the use of the chess game in *The Tempest*. We get a trope late in the play that enables us to rethink the action in these new terms.[8] And in these terms we are made aware of how deeply the sin of self-interest runs in both the Trojan and Greek societies. As both the Trojan and Greek council scenes in the first Act dramatize, so the battlefield scenes dramatize, namely, that the play explores the kind of mentality that makes war possible and insures its continuance.

From a major perspective, the obligatory scene in *Troilus and Cressida* is that between Achilles and Hector. We get it here. When in V.ix the soldiers all announce that, "Achilles! Achilles! Hector's slain! Achilles!" (V.ix.3), Diomedes clarifies the announcement with, "The bruit is, Hector's slain, and by Achilles" (V.ix.4). But we know not only that Hector has been murdered but also that Achilles has been likewise murdered: by entering the battle over the loss of his friend, Achilles has been drawn into the conflict, which will result in his own death by Paris. In a sense, the irony is that Hector exhausts himself on the sumptuous armor. He discovers that what he coveted covered death.

* * *

The play ends as it begins, with a speech addressed to us: we are first presented with a prologue; we are last given an epilogue.[9] Pandarus returns to the play in Act V just before the battle (V.iii) and right after it (V.x). Pandarus is now the essential choric figure, as was the Prologue at the beginning. In V.iii Pandarus enters with a letter from Cressida for Troilus; Pandarus's entrance in V.iii is therefore an end of the Troilus and Cressida action in the play. In V.x Pandarus enters after the battle, after Troilus has been tested on the battlefield. In each case Pandarus enters at the end of an action. His entrance, therefore, is a kind of an epilogue to that action. He comes in at the end of the private action, the love issue in the play, and he comes in at the end of the public action, the war issue in the play. But in V.x Pandarus is a real epilogue. He addresses the audience.

The most obvious feature of Pandarus's last speech is the verse. By reciting the verse in V.x, Pandarus is recalling his song in III.i. Pandarus's epilogue in V.x echoes his song in III.i. The song in III.i is "*Love, love, nothing but love*" (III.i.110). As we have seen, it is sung in the context of the trope of the bee. In V.x Pandarus's verse re-introduces the trope of the bee, only instead of the sweetness and light associated with the bee, Pandarus now speaks of the sting. In III.i the emphasis is on sweetness and "notes," song; in III.ii, IV.i, and IV.v the emphasis is on light and revelation. In V.iii the emphasis is on the loss of honey; now the emphasis is on the sting of the battlefield and the loss brought by it:

> Full merrily the humble-bee doth sing
> Till he hath lost his honey and his sting;
> And being once subdu'd in armed tail,
> Sweet honey and sweet notes together fail.
> (V.x.42-45)

The emphasis is thus on, as we might expect, the love plot. Troilus is now a savage. Aeneas will now be released. Pandarus soon will be dead. These three characters thus constitute three endings: Troilus, Aeneas, Pandarus.[10] We perhaps may say that these represent the head, heart, and hand. All have failed. Power, love, and wisdom have all proved to be ineffective. But we ought to extend the implications to Hector and, perhaps, to Achilles and Ajax: they too have been subdued in this "armed tale." Achilles has been brought into the conflict by the death of Patroclus. Only with the fall of Troy will anything positive result. This will be accomplished not when love comes to power and wisdom, as we have seen, but when power and wisdom come to love. The Trojan horse will lead to

Troy's fall. Then and only then can Aeneas, the son of Venus, be released to lead to Rome and through Rome to Christianity, which is a higher expression of love than Troy represents, an expression of love that corrects the sin of self-interest and turns commodity into comedy.[11]

The tension at the end of the play is not outside-inside, as is indicated by the offstage correlative action in V.vii, but "endeavour" and "performance," or what one wishes to do and what one accomplishes. Thus V.x is a version of V.vii, with a difference. The character equations are evident: Achilles and Hector; Menelaus and Paris and Troilus and Diomedes; Thersites and Pandarus. Troilus endeavors to love Cressida, but he does not perform what he promised. Aeneas endeavors to serve Hector well, but he ends up getting Hector killed. Pandarus endeavors to serve Cressida and Troilus, but he ends up helping to destroy them. Thus in the last scene of the play all appears disastrous. While Pandarus bequeaths us his disease,[12] we are wise to recognize the *dis-ease* at the end of the play. Still, it is useful to note that in the final scene Aeneas would "starve . . . out the night" (V.x.2), but Troilus saves Aeneas by leading him from the battlefield. As in I.i these two, Troilus and Aeneas, leave the stage together only now to seek safety for the night. Such safety will enable Aeneas, the true son of Venus, to survive the conflict and lead from Troy to Rome where a higher expression of love than what Troy represents can and will come to be.

Pandarus's last speech has fourteen rhymed lines:

> Let me see:
>   Full merrily the humble-bee doth sing
>   Till he hath lost his honey and his sting;
>   And being once subdu'd in armed tail,
>   Sweet honey and sweet notes together fail.
> Good traders in the flesh, set this in your painted
> cloths:
>   As many as be here in Pandar's hall,
>   Your eyes, half out, weep out at Pandar's fall;
>   Or if you cannot weep, yet give some groans,
>   Though not for me, yet for your aching bones.
>   Brethren and sisters of the hold-door trade,
>   Some two months hence my will shall here be made.
>   It should be now, but that my fear is this:
>   Some galled goose of Winchester would hiss.

> Till then I'll sweat and seek about for eases,
> And at that time bequeath you my diseases.
>
>   (V.x.41-57)

Because this speech contains fourteen rhymed lines, I should like to suggest that it is like a sonnet. As we have seen, Pandarus alerts us to the importance of rhyme in IV.iv:

> O heart, heavy heart,
> Why sigh'st thou without breaking?
>
> where he answers again
>
> Because thou canst not ease thy smart
> By friendship nor by speaking.
>
> There was never a truer rhyme. Let us cast away
> nothing, for we may live to have need of such a
> verse: we see it, we see it. How now, lambs?
>
>   (IV.iv.15-22)

Whereas the Prologue addresses us as "fair beholders" (26), Pandarus now addresses us more narrowly as "Brethren and sisters" (V.x.52). Thus Pandarus is addressing only part of the audience, his audience. Because, as we have seen, part of the play's difficulty is its shifting perspectives, as Kenneth Muir suggests,[13] not only does Pandarus have his audience but Aeneas has his audience and Troilus has his audience, too. Part of the difficulty of the enigmatic end of *Troilus and Cressida* is that each of the remaining characters has a special audience. Pandarus's end is displayed; the other two, those of Troilus and Aeneas, are implied.

As in *The Tempest*, the emphasis at the end of *Troilus and Cressida* is on art. *The Tempest* ends with a prayer;[14] *Troilus and Cressida* ends with an enigmatic sonnet.[15] Both plays end with an epilogue. The bee is traditionally a symbol of the artist, and this symbol gives way in Pandarus's speech to "painted cloths" (V.x.46-47). The movement in Pandarus's last speech is from the humble-bee to traders then from traders to the brothers and sisters of the "hold-door trade" (V.x.52), which may also be read as the "hold-ore trade." This suggests the idea of process, as does the bee, and as did the Troilus trope in I.i of the baking of bread, which is also part of the digestion image of the Prologue. The process of the play has taken us to Troy. We have seen the problem of the play from the shifting perspectives of Troilus in I.i, of Cressida in I.ii, of Pandarus in III.i, of Achilles in III.iii, of Ulysses in IV.v, of Hector and Troilus in V.iii, of Thersites in V.iv and V.vii. At the end of the play we are presented with three endings, Troilus, Aeneas, Pandarus, symbolic versions of power, love, wisdom. Now, as Pandarus indicates, we leave Troy and, like a bee, return to the hive, which, in the end, is the theater[16] or the study in which we find ourselves, more fully aware of the human implications of this mythic material.

NOTES

1. Alice L. Birney maintains that "Thersites continues to be our 'glass' for observing and interpreting individual characters and actions" (*Satiric Catharsis in Shakespeare: A Theory of Dramatic Structure* [Berkeley: Univ. of California Press, 1973], 107). Considering how thoroughly Thersites discredits himself in Act V, however, I must assert that Thersites's judgment is highly questionable. See also E.M.W. Tillyard, *Shakespeare's Problem Plays*, (London: Chatto and Windus, 1961).

2. Thersites has been widely discussed. I disagree with Bertrand Evans who asserts that "Thersites is the strongest force of unity in the play; perhaps the sole unifying force" (*Shakespeare's Comedies* [Oxford: The Clarendon Press, 1960], 185). See also Robert Hillis Goldsmith, *Wise Fools in Shakespeare* (East Lansing, Michigan: Michigan State Univ. Press, 1963) and Birney, *Satiric Catharsis*.

3. See Elias Schwartz, "Tonal Equivocation and the Meaning of *Troilus and Cressida*" *Studies in Philology* 69 (1977): 317. He notes that the vision Thersites presents is both revolting and true. That we get the play from his perspective enables us to determine the complexity of Thersites's vision.

4. "Thersites' invective is emotionally charged with the satirically sharp and accurate character sketch" (Birney, *Satiric Catharsis*, 106).

5. Thersites "sees folly everywhere," writes G. Wilson Knight, "and finds no wisdom in mankind's activity" (*The Wheel of Fire* [London: Methuen, 1963], 57). Knight's comment is useful, but I would argue that Thersites cannot see wisdom because he has no wisdom. He is the cynic who, as Oscar Wilde might say, knows the cost of everything and the value of nothing.

6. In V.v, for instance, we hear of Patroclus's death. Nestor announces that Hector has slain Patroclus. The death of Patroclus brings Achilles into the battle. Hector kills Patroclus off stage while on stage at the beginning of V.v Diomedes orders the servant to take Troilus's horse to Cressida. Diomedes's possession of Troilus's horse is related to Hector's killing of Patroclus. In V.i Thersites calls Patroclus Achilles's "masculine whore" (V.i.16). It is a Renaissance commonplace that horse is a pun for whore. Troilus's horse is like Achilles's whore. The offstage correlative action in V.v suggests that Diomedes possesses Troilus's horse as Hector kills Achilles's whore.

7. See n. 1 chap. 3 above.

8. Hector's "Most putrefied core" (V.viii.1) is clearly related to Achilles's judgment of

Thersites: "thou core of envy" (V.i.4). In V.i Achilles's core of envy, Thersites, brings him the letter that persuades him not to go to battle. Hector's putrefied core is that which brings him to the end of his day's fighting and thus makes it possible for Achilles to destroy Hector.

9. For significant discussions of the end of *Troilus and Cressida*, see Ralph Berry, *The Shakespearean Metaphor: Studies in Language and Form* (Totowa: Roman and Littlefield, 1978); Walter C. Foreman Jr., *The Music of the Close: The Final Scenes of Shakespeare's Tragedies* (Lexington: The Univ. Press of Kentucky, 1978); M. T. Jones-Davies, "Discord in Shakespeare's *Troilus and Cressida*; or The Conflict Between 'Angry Mars and Venus Queen of Love'," *Shakespeare Quarterly* 25 (1974): 33-41.

10. R.A. Foakes suggests that the play has three endings, which, he argues, is "the most curious feature of *Troilus and Cressida*" (*Shakespeare: The Dark Comedies to the Last Plays* [London: Routledge and Kegan Paul, 1971], 46).

11. "The ultimate experience of the self-consuming, self-rejecting appetite is concentrated in the final scene. Aeneas, the voice of cool moderation, has a metaphor that hints at the coming phase in the play's progress . . . and Aeneas, who had signaled the end of Troilus' idyll, now heralds the reckoning to come" (Berry, *The Shakespearean Metaphor*, 85).

12. For a useful discussion of the disease and animal imagery in the play, see Brian Vickers, *The Artistry of Shakespeare's Prose* (London: Methuen, 1968).

13. See n. 1 chap. 3 above.

14. For comment on the "prayer" in *The Tempest*, see William B. Bache, *Design and Closure in Shakespeare's Major Plays: The Nature of Recapitulation*, (New York: Peter Lang, 1991), 382.

15. Whereas *Romeo and Juliet* begins with a sonnet, *Troilus and Cressida* ends with this enigmatic sonnet.

16. For a discussion of the theater imagery in the play, see Anne Righter, *Shakespeare and the Idea of the Play* (London: Chatto and Windus, 1962).

Conclusion

Troilus and Cressida remains a play of monumental difficulty. No reading of the play is definitive; the play must still be studied. As Harold Goddard reminds us, each time we read a Shakespeare play we must read with more care and more deeply. Although a critical vocabulary is not firm or agreed upon, the hope is that an examination of how a play means may lead to an understanding of what a play means or what meanings a play may suggest. At least the attention is on meaning and understanding, where it belongs.

I have tried to make clear some of the patterns, strategies, and systems in *Troilus and Cressida* that make the play what it is. Tropes are a large-scale means of enabling us to determine meaning. As we might expect, the major trope for understanding *Troilus and Cressida* is that of the Apple of Discord. Other tropes are in evidence: the Elizabethan fair, the bee with its honey and wax, the outside-inside trope. Indeed Troilus and Cressida themselves are to be used as a pair of spectacles to enable our understanding of the human implications of the Trojan War.

With the Trojan War as a subject, Shakespeare's primary structural device is the recapitulative scene, the scene from the perspective of one or more characters. As we might expect, the first two scenes present the strategy in its purest form. The following scenes work variations on the strategy.

As we might also expect, the Prologue to the play, a distinguishing feature, presents what I consider to be the second most important structural strategy. It is a choric strategy of prologues and epilogues, an elaborate procedure that, throughout the action, poses what is presented over against what is told. We readily see Pandarus and Thersites as the major participants in this prologue-epilogue pattern. But the full strategy is elaborate and pervasive.

The value and necessity of what can be called, for want of a better term, the rewritten or revised scene has never been fully recognized. To appropriate an Eliot expression, every scene of *Troilus and Cressida* is involved in every other scene; every scene is at the service of every other scene; every scene deliberately mirrors and echoes at least one other scene. The rules for the elaborate fashioning process are the basis of Shakespeare's art. This is what Una Ellis-Fermor says on the relationship between form and theme in *Troilus and Cressida*:

> they collaborate, not fortuitously, but intentionally, . . . the form illuminates and interprets the theme, is itself ordered by it, each being in some degree an aspect of the other, precisely as we expect in a play which is a major work of dramatic art.[1]

Criticism has only begun to glimpse the essence of the Shakespeare achievement. Alfred Harbage has remarked that "*Troilus and Cressida* had best be recognized as occupying a unique and mysterious place in the canon."[2] A generation later we may reasonably assert that the real truth is the opposite of what the world has proclaimed: *Troilus and Cressida* is in fact quintessential Shakespeare.

NOTES

1. Una Ellis-Fermor, *Shakespeare's Dramatic Art* (London: Methuen, 1980), 122.
2. Alfred Harbage, *Shakespeare and the Rival Traditions* (Bloomington: Indiana Univ. Press, 1952), 119.

Index